W9-CMQ-568

16 EXTRAORDINARY
AMERICAN
ENTREPRENEURS

NANCY LOBB

J. WESTON
WALCH
PUBLISHER

Portland, Maine

Photo Credits

Frederick Tudor	Dover Photo Archive
Biddy Mason	Department of Special Collections University Research Library, UCLA
Andrew Carnegie	Dover Photo Archive
Montgomery Ward	AP/WIDE WORLD PHOTOS
King Gillette	AP/WIDE WORLD PHOTOS
Henry Ford	Dover Photo Archive
Madam C.J. Walker	Madam Walker Theatre Center
James Rouse	AP/WIDE WORLD PHOTOS
Mary Kay Ash	AP/WIDE WORLD PHOTOS
John H. Johnson	AP/WIDE WORLD PHOTOS
Fred Smith	AP/WIDE WORLD PHOTOS
Robert Swanson	Roger Ressmeyer/©Corbis
Ben Cohen and Jerry Greenfield	Richard T. Nowitz/Corbis
Oprah Winfrey	AP/WIDE WORLD PHOTOS
Bill Gates	AP/WIDE WORLD PHOTOS
Jerry Yang	Courtesy of Bob Houser

1   2   3   4   5   6   7   8   9   10

ISBN 0-8251-3795-0

Copyright © 1998
J. Weston Walch, Publisher
P. O. Box 658 • Portland, Maine 04104-0658

Printed in the United States of America

Contents

Introduction

The lives of many American entrepreneurs have made a difference in the story of America. These are men and women of vision. They have seen opportunity where others saw none. They have kept going when others gave up. They have created new products and new ways of doing things. They have made the American dream come true.

In this book, you will read the stories of 16 of these people:

- Frederic Tudor, the man who harvested ice from the frozen ponds of the North and shipped it around the world.

- Biddy Mason, a former slave who became a wealthy land-owner and philanthropist in Los Angeles.

- Andrew Carnegie, who built one of the world's greatest steel companies and then spent the rest of his life giving his fortune away.

- Montgomery Ward, who created the first large-scale mail order business.

- King Gillette, a would-be social reformer who is remembered as the inventor of the safety razor.

- Henry Ford, champion of assembly line production, who drove his Model T into the hearts of Americans.

- Madam C.J. Walker, America's first female African-American millionaire, who helped to bring pride and self-determination to black women.

- James Rouse, a builder with a vision who changed the face of American cities.

- Mary Kay Ash, who created a huge cosmetics empire with a part-time female sales force.

- John H. Johnson, owner of a vast media empire, including *Ebony* and *Jet* magazines and Black Entertainment Television.

- Fred Smith, who created Federal Express, a firm that guarantees delivery of packages overnight.

- Robert Swanson, who created the first biotechnology company using gene-splicing techniques.

- Ben Cohen and Jerry Greenfield, ice-cream makers who use their business as a tool for social change.

- Oprah Winfrey, a TV talk show host who is among the world's richest entertainers.

- Bill Gates, founder of Microsoft and one of the richest men in the world.

- Jerry Yang, co-founder of Yahoo!, one of the most popular search engines used on the Internet's World Wide Web.

Frederic Tudor
the Ice King

In 1854, a southern gentleman wrote a letter on the subject of ice to the editor of *Scientific American*. In it, he said, "It would be a great favor to myself, as well as to thousands in the interior of the South, if you will, through your journal, make known a practical way of making man-made ice. This information would prove of vast value to the interior of the South."

The editors replied, "We do not know of any workable plan for producing ice except at an expense so great as to prevent its use for common purposes. If there was any person who could make ice cheaply, he would not be at a loss where to go make his fortune!"

Frederic Tudor

Fourteen years later, in 1868, the first factory for making ice was built in New Orleans. But it would be many years before artificially made ice was commonly available. Before that, natural ice was harvested from frozen northern ponds and shipped south. One of the greatest of the ice harvesters was Frederic Tudor, the Ice King.

Frederic Tudor was born into a wealthy Boston family in 1783. His father, William Tudor, had studied law with John Adams. During the Revolutionary War, he was George Washington's judge advocate general. The four Tudor brothers were expected to follow in their father's footsteps and attend Harvard. The three older brothers all did. However, young Frederic was a bit of a rebel. At the age of 13, he quit school. He became an apprentice in the spice business. He bought and sold tea, sugar, and other spices.

Frederic and his brother William liked to discuss possible ways to make their fortune in business. One day in 1805, they were discussing some far-fetched ideas. Frederic joked that ice taken from nearby Fresh Pond could be shipped to warmer places and sold at a huge profit. No one took his idea seriously. But the more Frederic Tudor thought about it, the more he thought this plan could work. He began looking into how it might be done.

Tudor explained his thoughts in a December 1805 letter to a cousin. He said, "The idea of carrying ice to warm climates will at first no doubt startle and astound you. But when you take into account the following I think you will cease to doubt the practicality of the thing...."

For in fact, as Tudor further explained, others had already carried ice on long voyages. An American captain had taken a cargo of ice from Norway to London "and realized a handsome profit notwithstanding he was detained a long time in settling with the custom house on account of duties." Other ships had taken ice to the Indies. Also, "ice creams were carried to Trinidad by the English when they owned that island...."

Tudor was a careful and thoughtful man. He kept an "ice house diary." In it he kept records of his progress with the project. He sent his brother William to Martinique to get exclusive rights to sell ice there. He also persuaded some friends to join him as partners. In this way he raised some money for the project.

Frederic Tudor's first ice shipment was 130 tons of ice sent to Martinique. A Boston newspaper recorded the 1806 event. "No joke. A vessel has cleared the Custom House for Martinique with a cargo of ice. We hope this will not prove a slippery speculation."

Tudor went to Martinique with his ice. He realized that no one there would know what to do with ice. He sold ice to the owner of the Tivoli garden and showed him how to make ice cream from it. The ice cream proved very popular and was all sold quickly. The rest of the ice was sold for making drinks cold.

The Martinique trip had been a small success. But before long all Tudor's inventory had melted. He was left $4,000 in debt. Unable to pay his debts, Tudor was nearly thrown into debtor's prison. Luckily for him, he was allowed to return home and work on the family farm to pay off his debts.

More problems arose. Tudor's father lost his fortune. The War of 1812 came along. Frederic Tudor could no longer travel to the Caribbean. The ice business was frozen in its tracks.

When the war ended in 1815, Tudor again began a major effort to get his business off the ground. He returned to Cuba and was awarded exclusive rights to sell ice there. He also began building up a demand for his product in the southern United States. In fact, he had to convince people that they wanted ice! Tudor told doctors that patients could be helped by ice packs. He talked about the value of ice in food preservation. He introduced ice cream to places that had never heard of it. To show people that some drinks taste better cold, he sold both cold and warm drinks for the same price. People quickly came to prefer their drinks cold.

By the mid-1820's, Tudor's business had improved. But he was still making little profit. By this time, he was shipping about 2,000 tons of ice a year out of Boston. It cost about 30 cents to cut and ship a ton (2,000 pounds) of ice. He could sell that ice for 10 cents a pound in the South. Clearly, there was big money to be made in the ice business.

But first a few chilling problems had to be worked out. There was no easy way to cut the big blocks of ice and lift them from the pond. A better method was needed to keep the harvested ice from melting. Ways to pack the ice for shipping needed improvement. Ship captains reported that the ice was hazardous when it slipped about in the cargo hold. All of these problems needed to be resolved fast. Other people were getting into the ice business, cutting into Tudor's profits.

Frederic Tudor began working on better ways to store his product. He tried storing it aboveground in icehouses. He tried putting it belowground in a sort of cave. He tried insulating the ice with straw, wood shavings, and sheepskins, among other things. He decided on a type of aboveground wooden building. He put sawdust between the blocks of ice to keep air away from the ice. Then the ice was further insulated with hay.

In 1825, Tudor met Nathaniel Wyeth. Wyeth had made a new kind of ice cutter. The cutter had two blades about 20 inches apart. Pulled by a horse, the device cut two parallel grooves in the ice. More grooves were cut parallel to the others. Then the horse was driven at right angles to the first cuts. The surface of the ice looked like a giant checkerboard. Then metal bars were placed into the cuts, and the blocks of ice were pried apart. This yielded blocks of ice cut in a regular size. The blocks of ice were floated to the edge of the pond. They were lifted out and stored in an icehouse.

Wyeth's invention greatly increased the ease of the cutting process. Tudor bought exclusive rights to Wyeth's ice cutter. Wyeth was made manager of the ice company. Now, Tudor could cut ice for only 10 cents a ton. With this advantage, he jumped ahead of his competitors.

In 1841, Tudor talked the Massachusetts legislature into chartering a railroad line from the shores of Fresh Pond to the docks at Charleston, South Carolina. The Charleston Branch Railroad carried its first shipment of ice in December 1841. A brochure for the railroad claimed that "ice contributes as much to refreshment in the South as coal does to comfort in the North."

It had taken many years of hard work and frustration. But Tudor's company was starting to make it big. In 1846, Tudor shipped 65,000 tons of ice out of Boston harbor. The port of Boston had been in trouble. It was rapidly losing trade to the larger port of New York. Tudor's business helped to save the port of Boston, making him a local hero.

Demand for ice was increasing. Tudor bought exclusive rights at a number of ponds. Among them was the famous Walden Pond so beloved by Henry David Thoreau.

Tudor began a system of ice cultivation. He made large numbers of artificial ponds on Fresh Pond Meadows. The ponds covered about 25 acres of land and had clay bottoms. The artificial ponds were dug lower than Fresh Pond. Therefore, they could be filled from Fresh Pond to any depth desired. The ponds were kept shallow so they would freeze readily. In this way, the ice could be harvested as soon as the water froze. The cost of making these artificial ponds was about $1,000 an acre, or $25,000 altogether. Tudor built more icehouses to store the ice until it was needed.

The demand for ice continued to grow. Carpenters built "refrigerators" out of wood. They were advertised as "producing a powerful effect with the least possible consumption of ice."

The use of ice to refrigerate food and drink was changing American eating habits. By the mid-1850's, iceboxes were common in middle-class homes. The iceman brought chunks of ice by horse and buggy to sell in towns across the country.

Wholesale food dealers made good use of ice too. They lined freight train cars with ice to keep their products cool. They used ice to ship fresh fruits and vegetables longer distances. Butchers built their own icehouses for storing meat.

By 1856, Tudor was shipping 146,000 pounds of ice south from Boston. His ice empire extended as far as China, the Philippines, and Australia. Speedy clipper ships were used to carry the ice around the world. Ships of the Tudor Line included the *Ice King*, the *Ice Land,* and the *Ice Berg*. Frederic Tudor died in 1864 at the height of the ice trade. Toward the end of his life, he was a powerful man in his community.

Frederic Tudor was the Ice King. He made his fortune selling a resource abundant in the northern climates to lands farther south. He created a demand for his product where no demand had existed. While the need for ice shipments ended with the advent of modern refrigeration, Tudor's ice filled a need for a century.

Remembering the Facts

1. Frederic Tudor was an apprentice in what business?

2. How did Frederic Tudor come up with the idea of shipping ice from cold to warm climates?

3. Where did Tudor send his first shipment of ice?

4. Why did Tudor almost land in debtor's prison?

5. How did Tudor store his ice to keep it from melting?

6. How did Wyeth's ice cutter help Tudor make greater profits?

7. Why was Tudor thought of as a hero in Boston?

8. What is ice cultivation?

9. How did the use of artificial ponds increase the amount of ice available for sale?

10. How could ice be shipped as far away as China?

Understanding the Story

11. What types of changes do you think the availability of ice made in the lifestyle of the average American?

12. How do you think the availability of ice and refrigeration improves the health of the average American?

Getting the Main Idea

Why do you think Frederic Tudor was important in the history of American business?

Applying What You've Learned

Imagine that you live in a warm climate before ice or refrigeration was available. Make a list of ways your diet would be different than it is today.

Biddy Mason
Philanthropist

Biddy Mason, slave and midwife, walked 2,000 miles across the United States to California. There she became a powerful force in the young town of Los Angeles. Saving her small wages, she bought property in what would later be downtown Los Angeles. She became very wealthy. She used her money to help the poor and needy of all races.

Biddy Mason

Biddy Mason was born a slave on August 15, 1818, in the deep South, probably in Georgia. Her parents are not known. However, records show that she was part African American and part Native American. She was named Bridget, but she became known as Biddy at a young age.

Biddy grew up as a slave on a Mississippi plantation. She was owned by Robert and Rebecca Smith. She was trained to help the house servants and the midwife on the plantation. When she grew older, Mason managed the business affairs of the plantation. She also cared for Rebecca Smith, who was often ill.

Biddy Mason had three children, all girls. The girls' father was said to be Robert Smith, her owner.

In 1847, Robert Smith became a Mormon. He decided to move to the Utah territory. There the Mormons were building a home for themselves. On March 10, 1848, the Smith family and some other Mormons began the long journey to the Salt Lake Valley. Their slaves went along, including Biddy Mason. It was a grueling journey, taking almost a year. The white folks traveled by wagon. Biddy and the other slaves had to walk behind the caravan. They made the whole journey on foot.

Biddy organized the camp of 56 whites and 34 blacks every night. She herded the oxen, cows, and mules. She prepared meals for the group. At the same time, she took care of her own children, who were 10, 4, and newborn. Mason also acted as midwife for several births that took place along the route. Clearly, she was a woman of unusual endurance and strength.

The Smith family and their slaves lived in the Salt Lake Valley for three years. Biddy was not happy living among the Mormons. That group believed strongly that black people were a lesser race. In 1851, the Mormon leader Brigham Young asked for volunteers to start a new town in California. Robert Smith decided to go. He left Salt Lake City in 1851, taking his slaves with him.

It was to be another long trip on foot. The group was forced to camp at the Cajon Pass for three months until the weather was good enough to make it through the mountains. Finally, they arrived in San Bernardino, California.

Robert Smith must not have known that the California Constitution outlawed slavery. California had been admitted to the Union as a free state in 1850. Even so, no one was sure what the law meant to black people who were already slaves when they entered the state. Were they still slaves? Or were they free?

Robert Smith decided to take no chances on losing his slaves. He made plans to move to Texas with his slaves, including Biddy Mason and her three daughters.

When she learned of this plan, Mason was alarmed. She did not want to be forced to leave California for slavery in Texas. Biddy talked about her fears to Charles Owens, the young man her oldest daughter, Ellen, was dating. Charles did not want to lose Ellen. He told his father, Robert Owens, what was happening.

Robert Owens was an influential black businessman. He organized a petition which was presented to Judge Benjamin Hayes.

Judge Hayes placed Biddy and her daughters in protective custody. He wanted to guard them from Smith until the matter was settled.

It is hard to imagine the courage it took for Biddy to challenge her owner in court. If she had lost the case, she would most certainly have suffered greatly at his hands. During the trial itself, Biddy could not speak on her own behalf. A law forbade the testimony of a "colored" person against a white person. Luckily, Robert Smith failed even to show up for the trial. On January 21, 1856, Biddy Mason and her daughters were granted their freedom. The lawsuit set a legal precedent for the rights of black Americans in the new territories of the West.

Robert Owens then asked Biddy Mason and her daughters to live with him and his family until they got settled. She accepted. Not long afterward, Ellen Mason and Charles Owens were married.

Biddy Mason became a nurse and midwife for Dr. John S. Griffin. The two served women of all races and all social classes in Los Angeles and other nearby towns. Biddy soon gained a reputation as a skilled nurse and midwife. She delivered hundreds of babies for leading families, as well as for the needy. She became a figure known to all, as she walked down unpaved streets carrying her large black medical bag.

Biddy saved much of her wages of $2.50 per day. Ten years after gaining her freedom, she bought a large piece of land on Spring Street for $250. At that time, it was a bit out of town, but it would later be the heart of downtown Los Angeles. She called the land "the Homestead." Biddy Mason told her children that this piece of land should always remain their home. She thought of the land as a secure economic base for her family.

For the next 18 years, Biddy did not live on the land but rented a small house nearby. She was saving money to build a larger building on her land. Her plan was to live in part of the building and rent out the other space.

Biddy's purchase proved to be a wise investment, just as she had hoped. As the city grew, the land became more valuable. By the 1880's, Mason's block had changed from a rural area of small homes and vineyards to a dense business district. The main financial district of Los Angeles was located just south of her property.

By 1884, Biddy had sold a small part of her land for $1,500. She built a commercial building on another part. It had storerooms on the ground floor for rental.

She also allowed her grandsons to build a livery stable on the property. Later, she deeded them that part of her land. She moved into the apartment on the second floor in 1884. By this time, she was 66 years old.

Since the location of her land was excellent, Biddy Mason became wealthy. Over time, she bought more property, and her wealth grew. She bought four additional downtown lots for $375. In 1884, she sold one of these lots for $2,800, a great profit! It was clear to Mason that buying and renting out land in good locations was a good source of wealth.

But Biddy Mason's land was a source of wealth for more than herself. She used much of her profits to fund the work she was doing for the needy. In 1884, after she had sold the lot for $2,800, she gave orders to a neighborhood grocery store to open accounts for needy families in the area. Some families had become homeless after some flooding, so she helped them out with food.

She also used her land as a safe haven for the poor and distressed. Stranded settlers learned they could get aid from Biddy Mason. Often there were long lines of people looking for her help at 331 South Spring Street. Biddy never turned away a needy person of any race.

Biddy Mason was also a frequent visitor to the jails. She let prisoners know they had not been abandoned. She likewise brought gift of compassion and love to the ill and the insane in hospitals. She also set up day care for children of working parents.

Biddy was a religious woman. She was a founding member of the First African Methodist Episcopal Church in 1872. In fact, it was organized in her living room. She gave generously to the outreach programs of the church. She also paid the taxes on the church property, as well as the minister's salary. Biddy Mason was quoted as saying, "If you hold your hand closed, nothing good can come in. The open hand is blessed, for it gives abundance, even as it receives."

Biddy Mason died on January 15, 1891. Even on that day, a long line of people were standing outside awaiting her help. She was deeply mourned by the community she had served so well for more than 40 years. Yet, ironically, she was buried in an unmarked grave. It remained unmarked for almost 100 years. On Palm Sunday, March 27, 1988, a large tombstone to mark her grave was dedicated by the Mayor of Los Angeles plus nearly 3,000 members of the First African Methodist Episcopal church that Mason helped to found.

November 16, 1989, was declared Biddy Mason Day. At a ceremony at the Broadway Spring Center, a memorial to Biddy Mason's lifetime achievements was unveiled. It is a time line wall 8 feet high and 81 feet long in showing the major events in her life. Her original homestead has also been preserved at this site.

Biddy Mason's life had been a long journey. Not only had she traveled great distances across the United States, but she had made a place for herself and her family in a new land. She had made a lasting impression on the economic, health-care, and spiritual development of Los Angeles.

Remembering the Facts

1. What type of work was Biddy Mason trained to do on the plantation?

2. Why did Robert Smith decide to move his family and slaves to Utah in 1848?

3. Name three jobs Mason was assigned on the trip to Utah.

4. Why did Robert Smith decide not to stay in California?

5. How did Biddy Mason win her freedom?

6. What work did Biddy do after she was freed?

7. How did Biddy become wealthy?

8. Why did long lines of needy people form outside Biddy's homestead every day?

9. What church did Biddy help found?

10. What tribute to Biddy was unveiled on Biddy Mason Day in 1989?

Understanding the Story

11. Why do you think it took great courage for Biddy Mason to fight for her freedom?

12. Why do you think Biddy was able to become very wealthy?

Getting the Main Idea

Why do you think Biddy Mason was beloved by the people of Los Angeles?

Applying What You've Learned

Imagine that you are the historian assigned to create a time line mural depicting the major events in the life of Biddy Mason. Choose at least eight events in her life that you would include on the time line.

Andrew Carnegie
Steel Industrialist

The story of Andrew Carnegie is one of the great American success stories. Carnegie came to America from Scotland as a boy of 12. The boy's first American job paid him $1.20 a week. He went on to build one of the world's greatest steel companies. Retiring at the age of 65, he spent the rest of his life giving away his vast fortune.

Andrew Carnegie was born in Dunfermline, Scotland, on November 25, 1835. His father wove fine linen in the ground-floor room of the family home. The family lived in one room upstairs. His brother Tom was born when Andrew was eight years old.

Andrew Carnegie

Carnegie started school at eight. When he learned enough math, he kept his father's accounts. He also did his share of the chores. One of these chores was finding greens to feed the family's many rabbits. Carnegie came up with a plan to make the job easier. He promised his friends that if they gathered the greens, he would name a baby rabbit after each of them. His friends pitched in eagerly. This taught Carnegie a lesson he used all his life. People will work hard if they feel a personal stake in the job.

During Carnegie's youth, the Industrial Revolution was sweeping the world. A linen factory could hire unskilled workers to tend its machines. It could turn out linens faster and more cheaply than a hand weaver could. Weavers such as Carnegie's father were forced out of business.

Things were bleak. Finally, in May 1848, the family left their home. They sailed for America. It took the family three months to get to Pittsburgh. William Carnegie went to work in a cotton mill. He took 12-year-old Andrew along. Young boys were needed to work as "bobbin boys" for $1.20 a week. Andrew's job was to replace the bobbins as needed. (Bobbins are large spools holding the thread used by the looms.) There were no child labor laws at that time. So boys like Andrew Carnegie worked 12 hours a day, 6 days a week.

In 1850, an opportunity arose. Andrew Carnegie seized the chance to leave his dreary job. A new technology, the telegraph, was taking the country by storm. A telegraph company needed trained operators who knew Morse code. It also needed boys to deliver the telegrams (messages) it received. Carnegie got wind of a company that was going to be hiring a telegram boy. He applied for the job. He was too young and too small, and he didn't know the streets of Pittsburgh. But Andrew Carnegie convinced the owner that he was the man for the job! At a salary of $2.50 a week, Andrew Carnegie thought he had it made!

As a telegram boy, Carnegie had the chance to see businesses, offices, and homes he would never have otherwise seen. He met many important people. Soon he had learned Morse code. He was promoted to work as an operator.

In 1853, Carnegie left the telegraph company. He went to work for one of the men he had met as a telegram boy, Thomas Scott of the Pennsylvania Railroad. Carnegie worked at a variety of jobs for the railroad. In 1859, at the age of 24, he became the superintendent of the Western Division. He was earning $125 a month. This put him firmly in the upper middle class.

In 1861, the Civil War began. Scott and Carnegie were called to Washington, D.C. President Lincoln wanted them to organize the telegraph and railroad systems of the Union to help the war effort. Andrew Carnegie had been firmly opposed to war all his life. However, he felt it vital to preserve the Union. He organized a 1,500-man Telegraph Corps. The Corps helped the Union army maintain communications during the war.

During the war years, he also began investing in a variety of ventures. All of these paid off well. Saving his earnings from the railroad company, he invested in a new idea: Pullman sleeping cars. When these were adopted by all the railroads, Carnegie made a lot of money from his investment. He also invested in oil wells, an idea far ahead of its time.

Carnegie saw another investment opportunity in bridges. At that time, most bridges were made of wood. They often collapsed or caught fire when trains passed over them. Many people did not think that iron bridges could support a train. However, Carnegie knew they were often used in England. He founded the Keystone Bridge Works. It became a dominant force in American bridge building. The most famous bridge it built was the Brooklyn Bridge, the longest suspension bridge in the world at that time.

In March 1865, Carnegie quit his job with the Pennsylvania Railroad. He was making more money from his other ventures. Plus, he enjoyed being his own boss. In 1867, Carnegie moved to New York City, the financial capital of the country. Carnegie needed to make more business contacts for his business to grow.

Carnegie had a fine reputation in business circles already. A large part of his genius was his ability to work well with other men. Another of Carnegie's strengths was his firsthand knowledge of the inner workings of the new industries, such as the telegraph, the railroads, and the iron mills. Carnegie was so well regarded and well liked that people almost forced money on him to invest in his businesses.

Carnegie knew that most of his ventures depended on iron. In 1870, he decided to focus on being an "ironmaster." He decided to "put all good eggs in one basket and then watch the basket."

Carnegie soon found waste in the iron manufacturing process. No one was paying any attention to the amount or cost of the raw materials used. No one knew which work crews had produced more than others. Carnegie introduced a system called "cost accounting." This let him know the cost of each phase of his operation. Now there could be closer control over each step of the process.

It soon became clear that iron had limitations. Iron train tracks wore out quickly and had to be replaced every two or three months. Steel was both harder and more malleable than iron. (It could be hammered into thin sheets without breaking.) But it was very expensive to make. The introduction of the Bessemer process allowed steel to be made fairly cheaply. Carnegie knew this was an important innovation. He exclaimed, "The day of iron has passed. Steel is king!"

In 1873, Carnegie began building the largest steel mill in America. The site was 12 miles outside of Pittsburgh. By 1890, Carnegie Steel Company was the largest iron and steel producer in the world.

So much depended on steel. The railroads, which were being built at a phenomenal rate across the United States, used huge amounts of steel. Cities were building subways and skyscrapers. Farmers used machinery made of steel. Factories needed steel for their machines. Bicycles, ships, typewriters, and motor vehicles all required steel. Carnegie's empire of steel grew. He was worth half a billion dollars.

Several factors led to Carnegie's success. Because Carnegie treated his employees well, they were loyal and willing to work hard. He did not believe in selling stock in his companies. Thus, he could take all his company's profits and reinvest them. This made his profits grow more quickly. He cut waste by cost accounting. And he sold his product more cheaply than the competition. So everyone bought from him!

In 1900, Carnegie made a surprise move. He agreed to sell his company to J.P. Morgan for $480 million. Carnegie was then the richest man in the world! Next, he had to figure out what to do with all that money. Carnegie believed that "the man who dies with his fortune still intact, dies disgraced."

Carnegie believed that ignorance was at the root of social problems. Thus, one of favorite public causes was building libraries. Carnegie wanted his libraries to be free and open to the public. Any town that wanted a public library merely had to fill out an application. Carnegie would then give the town money to build the library. The town had to promise to buy the books and maintain the library. By the time he died, Carnegie had paid to build 2,811 libraries across the United States.

Church organs were another of Carnegie's favorite causes. A church had only to apply to Carnegie, and he would send the money. Carnegie paid for about 8,000 organs in all. Another gift to the world of music was Carnegie Hall in New York City. It is one of the finest concert halls in the world.

Carnegie gave generously to schools and colleges. He founded Carnegie-Mellon University in Pittsburgh. Today, it is a leader in computer and engineering fields.

Another of Carnegie's causes was the Hero Fund. This fund gave money and a Carnegie medal to people who risked or gave their lives to save others.

After 10 years of giving his money away, Carnegie still had $180 million left. He was 76 years old. He was afraid he might be running out of time. So he set up the Carnegie Corporation and turned the rest of his fortune over to it. He left a modest $15 million for his wife and daughter. Carnegie's "foundation" was to give away only the interest earned by his initial gift. In this way Carnegie could go on giving forever. This was a new way for the wealthy to dispose of their fortunes. Many wealthy people since then have followed this plan.

Carnegie also gave much time to his personal life. Devoted to his mother, he supported her. He did not marry until she died, when he was in his 50's. He and his wife had one daughter, who was born when Carnegie was 62.

Andrew Carnegie died on August 11, 1919. When his will was read, the world was astonished to learn that the richest man in the United States had succeeded in giving away nearly all of his vast fortune.

The death of Andrew Carnegie marked the end of an era in American history. He was an immigrant boy who arrived penniless and obtained great wealth and power. He symbolized the American Dream.

Remembering the Facts

1. What effect did the Industrial Revolution have on Andrew Carnegie's father?

2. What was Andrew Carnegie's first job in America?

3. What did the lack of child labor laws in the 1800's mean to the lives of the children of that day?

4. How did Carnegie's work as a telegram boy give him a unique opportunity to better himself?

5. Why did Carnegie leave the Pennsylvania Railroad, where he had an excellent job and good prospects for advancement?

6. Why did Carnegie become an ironmaster?

7. Why did Carnegie begin manufacturing steel?

8. Why was there such a huge demand for steel around the world?

9. Why did Carnegie begin giving his money away after he sold his company?

10. Why did Carnegie set up the Carnegie Corporation of New York when he was 76 years old?

Understanding the Story

11. Why do you think Carnegie's system of "cost accounting" would make a business run more efficiently?

12. Carnegie believed that "the man who dies with his fortune still intact, dies disgraced." Do you agree or disagree? Give reasons for your answer.

Getting the Main Idea

Why do you think it is often said that Andrew Carnegie's life symbolizes the American Dream?

Applying What You've Learned

Imagine that you have $1 billion to give away to worthy causes as you see fit (excluding yourself, family, and friends). Make a list of groups or causes to which you will give money and how much each one will receive.

Montgomery Ward
Catalog Sales Wizard

Catalogs! Sometimes they overflow your mailbox. There are catalogs for food, clothing, and sporting goods. Other catalogs offer exotic items for high prices. Catalogs can be entertaining, a nuisance, or a necessity. But believe it or not, mail-order catalogs have not always been around. The first large mail-order business was started by Montgomery Ward in 1872.

Montgomery Ward

In 1946, Grolier Club published a list of the 100 American books that had most influenced American life. One book on the list was the Montgomery Ward catalog. The Club said, "The mail order catalog has been the greatest single influence in increasing the standard of American middle-class living. It brought wholesale prices to city and hamlet, to the crossroads and the prairies. It urged millions of housewives to bring into their homes... comforts which otherwise they could never have hoped for. And above all, it replaced sound quality for shoddy...."

Aaron Montgomery Ward was born in 1843 in Chatham, New Jersey. Later, the Ward family moved to Michigan. At 14, he left school to work as an apprentice. Later, he worked as a barrel maker and then in a brickyard. He wrote afterward, "I learned I was not physically or mentally suited for brick or barrel making."

At the age of 19, Ward began working in a general store. He soon became the manager. The next year he was hired by Marshall Field's department store. He worked there for the next two years.

Montgomery Ward took up work as a traveling salesman. A friendly man, he often talked with the people he met on his sales route. It did not take him long to see an important fact. People in rural areas had money to spend. But there were few places for them to shop. The country store with its cracker barrel and warm stove was a great spot for farmers to gather. But they complained about the high price charged for often shoddy goods. These stores were not such good places to shop.

Ward had the idea of selling goods by mail. He would base his business in Chicago. A city of around 200,000, it was the railroad and shipping center of the Midwest. Ward began preparing his first catalog in 1871. As he was about to launch his new business, the Chicago fire of 1871 swept through the city. Most of the town was destroyed. Montgomery Ward lost everything.

But Ward knew his idea was too good to let it go up in smoke. He asked some friends to help him start over. A total of $1,600 was raised to start the business. In 1872, Ward's catalog appeared. It was a single sheet of paper, listing 163 items for sale at low prices.

Most of the items on the list were priced at $1. For $1 you could buy many things: 12 yards of best quality prints (fabric), hoop skirts, bustles, cotton hose and wool socks, shawls and handkerchiefs, lace curtains, an ostrich plume and three bunches of "fine French flowers." Customers paid cash for their purchases at the time of delivery. (This was called cash on delivery.)

Ward knew that many customers would be afraid to buy from an unknown seller. So he promised "Satisfaction Guaranteed or Your Money Back" on all his goods. This policy was vital to Ward's success. It remains the company's way of doing business today.

Sales were good the first year. The next year, in 1873, the company was named supplier of the National Grange. The Grange was a powerful national farmers' group. Thus, the signing of this account was a real accomplishment. Since farmers were his main customers, sales rose rapidly. Ward catered to Grange members. He offered them 10 days' credit on their purchases. He advertised Montgomery Ward as the "Original Grange Supply House."

Twelve years after the first one-page catalog appeared, the catalog was 240 pages. It offered 10,000 items for sale. Sales were close to $1 million a year.

People loved getting their catalog in the mail. It brought hours of entertainment for rural families. Children played a game called "You think of it, Ward's has it." Adults enjoyed keeping up with what was new in the world of fashion. One customer recalled, "When I was a child, the arrival of Ward's catalog was like having Christmas come three or four times a year."

Montgomery Ward's catalog had a place in the schoolroom as well. It became a "McGuffey's reader" and dictionary in one. Teachers used the price lists to teach arithmetic. And if an object unfamiliar to students was mentioned in a lesson, out came the catalog. Usually, the object was there!

Montgomery Ward oversaw every step of the catalog operation. He wrote the entire catalog himself. His direct, folksy style became a big selling point. He carefully examined every product before he put it in his catalog. It was not uncommon for him to make comments in the catalog such as this note, listed under a picture of pots and pans: "Manufacturer's measure, will not hold quite as much as represented." People came to know that things in the Ward's catalog were just as described.

Ward hoped to help make farmers' jobs easier and faster. The catalog sold windmills, pumps, feed cutters, corn shellers, threshers, saws, steam engines, and more. For the farmer's wife, Ward's sold "Adjustable Animal Power." This was a treadmill operated by a farm animal to supply power for a butter churn or grindstone! The farmer's wife also loved her "New Home" sewing machine, which cost "half the retail price."

In 1899, Ward Tower was built on Michigan Avenue in Chicago. At 25 stories tall, it was then the tallest building west of Philadelphia. The Ward's catalog that year was 1,036 pages long. It featured a photo of Ward Tower on its cover. But by 1909, the company had outgrown Ward Tower. A huge mail-order house was built along the Chicago River.

By this time, there were other mail-order businesses. The largest of these was Sears, Roebuck and Co. which had moved to Chicago in 1893. A few years later, Sears had become Ward's biggest competitor. Still Montgomery Ward & Company was a huge business. It had 6,000 employees and $40 million in yearly sales.

Ward's was now among the largest customers of the post office. Since 1863, there had been free home delivery in most large towns. But rural folks had to pick up their mail from the nearest post office. So it was an important change when Rural Free Delivery became law in 1896. Mail was now delivered right to farmers' homes. It became easier than ever for farmers to order by mail. A second boon to mail-order houses came in 1913. Parcel post service greatly lowered rates for packages. Ward's was one of the very first businesses in Chicago to use the new service.

Not surprisingly, many small-town stores hated the giant catalog companies. Some got people to toss their catalogs into a bonfire. They offered prizes to the person who threw in the most catalogs. Other stores launched false attacks against Ward's. They said Ward's merchandise was stolen, made in prisons, or shoddy. Others threatened people who ordered from the catalogs. Ward's had to start mailing its catalogs in plain brown paper wrappers.

In the early 1900's, many employers exploited their workers. They offered only long working hours, low pay, and miserable working conditions. But Ward was more progressive. His company was clean and well lit. Ward's was one of the first companies to publish a company magazine. Its purpose was to promote goodwill among its employees. It was also the first major company to give its employees a group life insurance policy. The policy covered sickness, accidents, and old-age benefits.

Ward was an early environmentalist. His biggest project was his fight to preserve the lakefront opposite Chicago's downtown area as a park. Over a 20-year period, Ward fought in the courts. He knew that once businesses were allowed to locate on that strip of land, it would be lost forever. Ward spent $200,000 in court costs. Finally, he won his fight to preserve this beautiful open space. *The Chicago Tribune* later praised Ward saying, "Grant Park is Montgomery Ward's monument."

Montgomery Ward was a generous man. Each summer he placed an order with a local coal company to deliver coal to various needy people in town. The people were never told who had sent the gift. He also sent anonymous gifts of clothing and groceries to the homes of those in need.

In 1913, Montgomery Ward died. His business would undergo vast changes over the next century. These changes would have surprised and disappointed Ward.

In the 1920's, both Ward's and Sears saw that changes were needed. Fewer people were living on farms. Farm income was dropping. As more people owned cars, farmers could drive into town to shop. Both stores began to open chain stores. In 1926, the first Montgomery Ward store opened in Plymouth, Indiana. Many more would follow.

In 1939, Montgomery Ward advertising writer Robert May was asked to come up with something new for Santa Claus to hand out to children visiting their local Montgomery Ward's. He came up with the character and song "Rudolph the Red-Nosed Reindeer" to fill this assignment. Today, Rudolph is beloved by children (and adults) around the world.

After struggling during the Great Depression, the network of stores began to overshadow Montgomery Ward's catalog business. In 1985, the catalog sales were discontinued. Ward's had decided to concentrate on its retail stores. But Montgomery Ward's idea for a catalog business had not died. It had merely been transferred to hundreds of other entrepreneurs selling by mail.

The retail business is very competitive. Montgomery Ward & Company has found it difficult to compete with other giant retailers. In July 1997, the company filed for reorganization under Chapter 11 of the United States Bankruptcy Code. This move will give the company time to regroup. Whatever the future holds, Montgomery Ward and his catalog were an important part of America's business history.

Remembering the Facts

1. How did Ward begin his career in retailing?

2. Name three reasons people in the early American West were not satisfied with the general stores.

   (a)

   (b)

   (c)

3. What happened to Ward's first attempt at a catalog business?

4. Describe the first Montgomery Ward catalog.

5. How did Ward make mail-order shopping worry free?

6. What account gave the Ward's catalog a huge boost in sales?

7. How did Rural Free Delivery help catalog sales?

8. What business was Ward's major competitor in catalog sales?

9. Why did Montgomery Ward begin opening chain stores?

10. How was the character "Rudolph the Red-Nosed Reindeer" developed?

Understanding the Story

11. Why do you think the Ward's catalog was such a treasure in the homes of many farm families in the early 1900's?

12. Why do you think Ward's dropped the catalog in 1985?

Getting the Main Idea

Why do you think Montgomery Ward and his direct-mail catalog business are an important part of America's business history?

Applying What You've Learned

Imagine that you are designing a catalog to show the resources of your school. What categories (for instance, courses, clubs, etc.) would you use to show the offerings of your school?

King Gillette
Inventor of the Safety Razor

King Gillette wanted to go down in history as a great social reformer. Instead, he is remembered as the inventor of the safety razor and its disposable blade. He brought about great changes in the daily lives of American men, just not in the way he planned. The Gillette Company has been a part of the American scene for nearly a century!

King Camp Gillette was born on January 5, 1855 in Fond du Lac, Wisconsin. He had two older brothers and four sisters. When King was four years old, the family moved to Chicago. The children went to public schools.

King Gillette

Gillette's parents were creative and energetic. His father owned a hardware store and worked as a patent agent. He was always tinkering with new inventions. He encouraged the boys to figure out how things worked. His mother wrote *The White House Cookbook*, a best-selling book of recipes and household hints. She was an inventive cook. Once she prepared a dinner of rattlesnake meat! It is no wonder that King Gillette grew up to be an imaginative thinker and inventor!

In 1871, a disastrous fire struck Chicago. Three hundred people were killed. Most of the city's buildings, which were made largely of wood, were destroyed. The Gillette family lost nearly everything they had. King Gillette was forced to quit school at the age of 16 to help support his family. He became a traveling salesman. In 1890, he married Atlanta Gaines. The couple later had one son.

This was a difficult time in American history. There was rapid industrial growth in the cities. Working and living conditions of many of the workers were miserable. Crime and poverty were widespread. There were conflicts between labor and management in factories. There were problems on the farms too. Many farmers were unable to sell their crops for enough money to survive.

Gillette spent a lot of time thinking about these problems as he traveled about the country, selling his wares. He wrote down his ideas and had them published in the book *The Human Drift* in 1894. His plan called for reorganizing the world into a giant corporation. This corporation would take over all the industries of the world. It would be owned and managed by the people, and everyone would work for the corporation. Everyone would be treated equally and receive equal benefits and pay. Thus, there would be no more crime or poverty. An earthly paradise (utopia) would reign.

Gillette's ideas were typical of socialism, a popular school of thought in America at the time. In a socialist system, land, transportation, natural resources, and industries are owned by the government. Socialists in Gillette's day were talking about ways a utopian society could be formed.

The Human Drift went largely unnoticed by the public. Gillette concluded that the problem was that he didn't have enough money to advertise the book. He decided that the best way to get the money would be to come up with an invention that would make him a fortune. All he needed was an idea for that invention!

William Painter owned one of the companies that Gillette worked for as a traveling salesman. Painter had invented a new kind of disposable bottle stopper. It was a cork-lined tin cap that could be crimped tightly over a bottle top. The cap soon became standard in the bottling industry. Painter became very wealthy.

Painter and Gillette were good friends. They often discussed the development of new inventions. One day, Painter said something that stuck in Gillette's mind. "King," he said, "you are always...inventing something. Why don't you try to think of something like the Crown Cork which, when once used, is thrown away, and the customer keeps coming back for more?"

Gillette did think about it. In fact, he became obsessed with the idea of inventing something that was disposable. Finally, in 1895, an idea came to him. Gillette later described this moment: "On one particular morning when I started to shave, I found my razor dull. It was not only dull but it was beyond the point of successful stropping. (A strop is a leather strap used for sharpening razors.) It needed honing, for which it must be taken to a barber or to a cutler. (Honing is sharpening a blade on a stone.) As I stood there with the razor in my hand, my eyes resting on it as lightly as a bird settling down on its nest—the Gillette razor was born. I saw it all in a moment. In that same moment many unvoiced questions were asked and answered with the rapidity of a dream rather than by the slow process of reasoning."

Abandoning his attempt to shave, Gillette went straight to the hardware store. He bought steel ribbon, pieces of brass, files, and a small vise. He began to make a model of his idea. And he wrote a letter to his wife, who was visiting family out of town. He said, "I have got it; our fortune is made."

Indeed, shaving at this point in history was still a difficult and time-consuming task. Men either used a straight razor or grew a beard (a popular choice). First, the razor blade had to be kept very sharp. The gentleman could hone it on a strop or a stone himself or take it to a cutler, who would do the job. Once the blade was sharp, the shave could begin. First, the man had to apply a soapy lather to his face to make the whiskers softer and easier to cut. Then he used the blade to scrape away the whiskers. Using a straight razor could be a dangerous process, especially if the man was a little clumsy or inexperienced. The first shave was a fearful rite of passage for a young man in his teens!

A good shave required not only skill but a lot of time as well (about 30 minutes). Men who could afford it often chose to have their shave at the barbershop. Obviously, this took a lot of time as well. As the pace of life began to quicken, the time was ripe for a faster, safer method of shaving. If he could perfect his idea, Gillette was almost sure of a winner.

Gillette's idea was not complicated. A sharpened steel blade would be fastened tightly between two metal plates. Enough of the blade would protrude to form a cutting edge. Yet the blade would be held in place at an angle that would make cuts unlikely. Gillette carved a model of his idea from a block of wood. On August 11, 1899, he applied for a patent on his idea.

However, it was one thing to show one handmade razor to the patent office. It was quite another to turn out the millions of blades needed to make the idea a commercial success. Also, the machinery to make the blades did not yet exist. Gillette had to find someone with the skills to make such a machine.

Gillette showed his idea to a machinist named William Nickerson. Nickerson made better models of the safety razor for Gillette to show potential investors. (Later, Nickerson came up with equipment that would produce the blades.) In 1901, Gillette convinced several friends to invest $5,000 in the project. The Gillette Safety Razor Company was born.

There were still many problems to overcome. A method had to be perfected for producing the type of steel needed for the blades. Once this was done, the blades had to be cut to fit the razor and honed to the desired sharpness. This honing was done by hand at first. Work on the project progressed slowly. Gillette was close to bankruptcy when he was able to persuade another group to invest $60,000 in the idea. This investment allowed him to finish the machinery needed to mass produce the razors and blades.

In 1903, the first Gillette razors were put on the market. The very next year, 90,000 razors and 12 million blades were sold.

Gillette poured his profits into advertising. He put his portrait on the wrapper of every blade. The first ads stressed the disposable aspect of the product: "No Stropping, No Honing." They also promised the customer 20 to 30 shaves per blade. Sales soared. King Gillette began making a large profit.

Readers of Gillette's socialist thoughts must have been surprised to see his picture in ads and on razor blade packages. They must have wondered if this was the same man who had written *The Human Drift* 10 years before. Yet, even as he was deeply involved in business, King Gillette had not given up his utopian ideas. He used much of his profits to publish more books about his ideas.

He hired a professional writer to help him write *Gillette's Social Redemption* in 1907 and *Gillette's Industrial Solution* in 1908. In 1910, Gillette wrote *The World Corporation*. In this book he explained how he hoped to establish his world corporation in the Arizona Territory. Gillette offered former president Theodore Roosevelt $1 million to be head of his corporation. (Roosevelt declined the honor.) The plan never came into being.

In 1910, Gillette sold most of his shares in Gillette Safety Razor Company to John Joyce for $900,000. Gillette kept the title of president. Joyce took over running the company. Gillette was free to spend his time working on his utopian ideas.

World War I firmly established Gillette razors in American homes. Military leaders liked their troops to be clean-shaven (for health reasons). Millions of soldiers were given Gillette razors by the U.S. government. For many, it was their introduction to shaving themselves. (Some even had to be instructed to remove the wrapping before trying to use the blade!) When the war ended, the Gillette Company had millions of loyal customers.

In the 1920's, the Gillette Company ran many promotions for their razors. Razors were sold in bulk to stores with instructions to give them away. Once customers had their free razor, they would buy the blades to use in it. Gillette also sent attractive young ladies to stores to conduct demonstrations of the correct way to use the razors. The Gillette Company used a lot of the profits to build new factories around the world.

King Gillette died in 1932. He had failed to make many of his social ideas reality. But his impact on the daily lives of American men was great.

Today, the Gillette Corporation offers many products, including deodorants, pens, batteries, toothbrushes, and so on. In 1997, it was ranked in the Fortune 500, a list of the largest companies in the United States. The Gillette Company has grown beyond the wildest dreams of the champion dreamer, King Gillette.

Remembering the Facts

1. How did King Gillette hope the world would remember him?

2. How did Gillette's mother show her creativity?

3. What effect did the Chicago fire of 1871 have on Gillette?

4. What kinds of problems had industrial growth in America created for workers?

5. In what 1894 book did Gillette introduce his idea of a world corporation?

6. Why did Gillette decide he needed to come up with an invention that would make a lot of money?

7. Name two reasons shaving with a straight razor could be a problem.

8. Once Gillette had designed a model of his idea for a razor, what was the next big hurdle to overcome?

9. What event in history made the popularity of Gillette razors soar?

10. Where did Gillette hope to build his world corporation, and who was to head it?

Understanding the Story

11. Some said Gillette seemed to live in two worlds: the world of dreams and the business world. How do you think he could have had such opposite sides to his personality?

12. It took eight years between the time Gillette had his idea for the safety razor (in 1895) and when the first razors were sold to the public (in 1903). Do you think this type of delay is common for inventions? Why or why not?

Getting the Main Idea

Why do you think King Gillette was not successful in getting anyone to do more than talk about his utopian ideas?

Applying What You've Learned

Imagine you are the marketing manager for Gillette razors. Think of a campaign to promote razor sales.

Henry Ford
Automotive Pioneer

Henry Ford, a pioneer of assembly-line production, drove his Model T straight into the hearts of Americans everywhere. His well-built, low cost car changed the lifestyle of the nation.

Henry Ford

Henry Ford was born on a 40-acre farm near Greenfield Village (now Dearborn), Michigan, on July 30, 1863. His parents were William and Mary Ford. When he was seven years old, he began attending school. Henry was too restless to be a good student. Reading and spelling were difficult for him, but he was good at math. After school, Henry did chores on the farm. He disliked farming, later saying, "Considering the results there is altogether too much work."

Henry loved machinery the way his brothers loved sports. Often he would walk all day to get to Detroit so he could visit hardware stores and look over the watchmaking tools. Everyone in his family thought he was strange, calling him "Crazy Henry." Only his mother understood him, praising him as a born mechanic. She encouraged his experimentation, even giving him her darning needles to make into screwdrivers for repairing watches.

His mother died when Henry was 12. He was devastated. He had lost the only member of his family who had understood him.

Henry's relationship with his father went downhill. William said of his son sadly, "He's not much of a farmer; he's a tinkerer." Henry paid less and less attention to his work at school and on the farm. He dreamed of the day he could build engines of his own.

In the fall of 1879, Henry told his father that he wanted to go to Detroit to get a job in a machine shop. William Ford was not happy; he still hoped Henry would help him on the farm. Finally William gave in. He hoped that Henry would find city life unappealing and soon return home.

Henry's first job was in the machine shop of Michigan Car Company, where he earned $1.10 a day (a high wage at the time). He kept this job only six days. In just an hour, he had repaired a machine the older mechanics had worked on all week. Apparently, they disliked being shown up by a 16-year-old. This experience taught Henry Ford "not to tell all you know."

Henry quickly got another job in the machine shop of the Flower Brothers. He was hired as an apprentice for $2.50 a week. Since he was paying $3.50 a week for room and board, he also worked at a watch repair shop to earn extra money. The owner of the repair shop hired Henry on one condition. He had to work in the back of the shop and come in by the side door. The owner was afraid his customers wouldn't leave their watches if they knew the age of his repairman.

Although Henry was a poor reader, he read everything he could find about engines. He was especially interested in gasoline engines, rather than the more popular steam engines.

Henry found a better paying job with the Detroit Drydock Company, the largest shipbuilding company in Detroit. For two years he worked there as a machinist. He continued to repair watches in the evenings.

In the spring of 1882, Henry went home to help his father on the farm and repair farm machinery in the area. That summer a neighboring farmer bought a portable steam engine from Westinghouse to do threshing and log sawing. The farmer knew little about machinery, so he hired Henry for $3 a day to run the machine. Henry traveled from one farm to another operating the machine. At the end of the summer, Westinghouse hired him to demonstrate their machines.

After this, Henry did no more farmwork. In the summers, he demonstrated Westinghouse engines. In winters he did experiments in a workshop on the farm. For Henry's 21st birthday, William Ford gave him a 40-acre piece of timberland. He told Henry that if he would cut the timber, the land was his. Henry did clear the land. And he stayed put for a little while, not because of the land but because he had met Clara Bryant. When he married her in 1888, the couple moved into a small house on the land.

One evening as they sat in their parlor, Henry said, "I've been on the wrong track. What I would like to do is make an engine that will run by gasoline and have it do the work of a horse." Grabbing a piece of paper, he sketched out his idea. He then told her he had been offered a job at the Detroit Edison Company. She agreed to leave the farm she loved and move to Detroit so he could pursue his dream.

In 1893, their son Edsel was born. Henry Ford was promoted to chief engineer of the Edison Company at a salary of $100 a month. He continued to work on his idea of a "horseless carriage" in the shed in his backyard. Many other inventors, all unknown to the public and each other, were working on designs for cars. By 1895, a few cars driven by gasoline motors were actually in operation in the United States.

By June 3, 1896, Ford's car was ready for a trial run. The car's body was mounted on four bicycle wheels with rubber tires. The car had two speeds and four horsepower. It had no brakes; to stop it, Ford killed the engine. There was no reverse gear. To go backwards, Ford got out and pushed the car backwards. But Ford's first car, which he called a quadricycle, was ready to go.

Ford had not thought of one problem: The car was too big to fit through the door of the shed. Henry Ford picked up an ax and begin knocking down the wall. Soon the car was out. It made a successful run around the block and back! After this, Ford often rode around the streets in his car, usually with a man riding a bicycle out in front to warn people with horses to "hold your horses."

In the meantime, Ford kept his job with the Edison Company. In 1896, the company sent him to a convention in New York. There he met Thomas Alva Edison, inventor of the light bulb. Ford explained his idea for a gasoline-powered car to Edison. Edison immediately grasped Ford's idea that gas was better than steam or electricity for running a car. "Young man," he said, "you have it. You don't have to carry water and coal for steam, and you don't have to be near a place to charge your batteries. You have a unit that carries its own fuel. Keep at it." This was the greatest moment in Ford's life. From then on, Thomas Edison was his idol.

In 1899, Ford left his job at the Edison Company. With the backing of several men, including the mayor of Detroit, he formed the Detroit Automobile Company. The short-lived company built a number of cars but collapsed in 1900, when the partners disagreed about what type of cars to build.

By this time a car was no longer seen as a futuristic dream. Four thousand cars had been built in America, most of them driven by steam engines. But interest was growing in the gasoline engine. Many inventors were racing to be the first to develop a practical gasoline-powered car.

Henry Ford needed to make a name for himself to attract investors for a new car company. He decided to build a race car. Ford drove his race car in a race at the Detroit fairground on October 10, 1901. He won first place, $1,000, and a crystal punch bowl. Ford found out he did not like racing! As he got out of the car, he was heard muttering "I'll never do that again! I was scared to death." He didn't have to. For the next race, he hired Barney Oldfield, a daredevil bicyclist, to drive. First, Oldfield had to learn to drive! He did, and a week later, Oldfield won the race with a new world-record time of 66 seconds for a mile. This win brought Ford the backing he needed to form the new Ford Motor Company in 1903.

Ford began making the Model A. Demand for the car was strong. However, Ford kept working on ideas for newer models, naming each model after the next letter of the alphabet. Ford was not yet satisfied. He knew that if he could make a low priced, reliable car, there would be no limit to the market for it.

He said, "I will build a car for the multitude. It will be large enough for the family but small enough for the individual to run and care for. It will be constructed of the best materials, by the best men to be hired, after the simplest designs that modern engineering can offer. But it will be so low in price that no man making a good salary will be unable to own one."

On March 19, 1908, the first ads came out for the Model T. It was a homely car, made beautiful by its simplicity, design, and power. The public loved it! The car quickly became the national mascot. It was given affectionate nicknames, such as "Tin Lizzie," "Leaping Lena," and "Galloping Snail."

In 1909, Ford declared that from then on his company would manufacture only the Model T, which would be available in any color the customer wanted, "as long as it is black." Ford had realized that "the way to make automobiles is to make... them all alike—just as one pin is like another."

Ford wanted to simplify his operation so his cars could be made more cheaply. Mass production methods were revolutionizing the manufacture of smaller items, such as guns. Ford thought of a way to use this technique to build cars. He built the largest plant in the country at Highland Park, Michigan. Conveyor belts took parts from one group of workers to the next. Each task was so simple that untrained workers could learn it quickly. Then they did the same job over and over. Where possible, machines replaced men.

The plan worked. Cars could indeed be made more cheaply. When the Model T was introduced in 1908, it sold for $850. The price kept dropping until in 1925, the car was sold for $240.

However, work on the assembly line was boring and exhausting. The men had to repeat their task at a fast rate like robots. It was hard to keep workers on the job. In 1914, Ford came up with a plan to help his workers. He would pay each worker $5 a day (double the going rate). He shortened the work day from 10 to 8 hours. His rivals thought Ford was crazy, but he replied, "I expect to get more efficient labor because living standards will be raised, and the men will be satisfied to work."

As his wealth grew, Ford wanted his company to make every part that went into his cars. He bought iron and coal mines, forests, mills, and factories. Later he built railroad and steamship lines and an air freight service to transport his products.

On May 25, 1927, Ford announced that no more Model T's would be made. The next day, car number 15,000,000 rolled off the assembly line. A few months later, the new Model A was introduced. Larger and more luxurious than the Model T, it was designed to keep up with the competition, like the Chevrolet. "Henry's made a lady out of Lizzie" was the going joke of the day.

Ford won fame for his philanthropic (charitable) works. He was also a pacifist (a person who is opposed to war). In 1915, he built a hospital in Detroit. During World War I, he headed a party of pacifists in a failed attempt to end the war. Nonetheless, his company profited greatly from both world wars, building ambulances and airplane engines, among other war materials.

In 1929, Henry opened Greenfield Village. Set on 254 acres, it is a model village that preserves the old ways. He had the houses of men he admired (such as Thomas Edison) transplanted and made part of the village. There were also vast displays relating to the history of the American automobile.

Henry Ford wanted his philanthropic work to continue after his death. To that end, he founded the Ford Foundation in 1936. He funded the foundation with both money and Ford Motor stock.

The foundation works for goals Ford supported in his lifetime. It funds programs that reduce poverty and injustice. It gives grants or loans to groups seeking to strengthen democratic values, promote international cooperation, and prevent war. It financially supports education, science, the arts, and culture.

In 1945, Ford passed the presidency of Ford Motor Company to his grandson, Henry Ford II. Henry Ford died on April 7, 1947, at the age of 83. Most of his personal estate, valued at $205 million, went into the Ford Foundation.

Today the assets of the Foundation have grown to more than $3 billion. It is one of the largest philanthropic trusts in the world. Henry Ford would be pleased to learn how his philanthropic work is continuing 50 years after his death.

Remembering the Facts

1. Why was the death of Henry's mother especially hard on him?

2. Why was Henry's father disappointed in him?

3. Name two of the mechanical jobs Henry Ford had in his teens.

4. Name two characteristics of Henry Ford's first car, the quad-ricycle.

5. Why did Thomas Edison become Ford's idol?

6. How did Henry Ford get the financial backing for the Ford Motor Company?

7. Why did the Model T achieve such popularity?

8. Why did Ford have trouble keeping workers at his automobile plant after he began the assembly lines?

9. Why did Henry "make a lady out of Lizzie"?

10. Why did Ford buy railroads, coal mines, and forests?

Understanding the Story

11. Why do you think Ford was able to drop the price on his Model T from an initial price of $850 down to $240?

12. Why do you think Henry Ford's father (who died in 1905) was unable to see the worth of his son's mechanical genius?

Getting the Main Idea

It has been said that Henry Ford changed the lifestyle and economy of America. Why do you think this is true?

Applying What You've Learned

Imagine that you are a consultant on a team that is designing a new car for the teenage market. Make a list of some features you would suggest for a car that would appeal to teens. Pick a name for the car.

Madam C.J. Walker
Hair-Care Innovator

Madam C.J. Walker was born poor, but she became America's first female African-American millionaire. She never forgot her roots. Madam Walker helped thousands of African-American women develop pride in themselves while they earned the money to provide for their children. Madam Walker used her fortune to help her community and taught others to do the same.

Madam C.J. Walker

Madam C.J. Walker was born Sarah Breedlove on December 23, 1867, in a one-room cabin on a cotton plantation near Delta, Louisiana. Her parents and older brother and sister were all slaves until 1865. Sarah was born free. Since her parents could find no other work, they kept working in the cotton fields for their former owners.

There were few schools for black people. Sarah began working in the cotton fields when she was five years old.

On Saturdays, Sarah, her mother, and sister did wash for white people, who paid them about $1 a week. Washing was hard work. The clothes had to be boiled in huge pots and then hung up to dry. Large items, like sheets and tablecloths, were very heavy when soaking wet. The strong soap the women used contained lye, a good cleaner, but hard on the hands. It was backbreaking work, but they needed the money.

In 1874, yellow fever struck the town of Delta. Many lives were lost, including those of seven-year-old Sarah's parents. The three children were left alone. Sarah's brother moved to Vicksburg to find work. Sarah and her sister tried to support themselves with their washtubs.

The girls moved across the river to Vicksburg, hoping to find work. Sarah's sister married a bad-tempered man who treated Sarah badly. When Sarah was 14, she married Moses McWilliams, a Vicksburg laborer.

When Sarah was 17, she had a child whom she named Lelia. When Lelia was just two years old, Moses was killed in an accident. At 19, Sarah McWilliams was left a widow with a small child to support. She couldn't imagine how she would survive. Friends told her that washerwomen were better paid in St. Louis. So, Sarah boarded a steamboat bound for St. Louis with her baby on her hip.

At that time, St. Louis was the third largest city in the United States. It also had a large African-American community. Sarah McWilliams found a room. She sent her daughter to school. Sarah worked all day washing clothes to support them.

As she worked, Sarah thought to herself, "As I bent over the washboard and looked at my arms buried in the soapsuds, I said to myself, 'What are you going to do when you grow old and your back gets stiff?' This set me to thinking. But with all my thinking, I couldn't see how I, a poor washerwoman, was going to better my condition."

Sarah continued to work long, hard hours. She made very little money. But each week she put a little of it aside. When Lelia graduated from high school, Sarah was able to send her to college.

Sarah always wore older clothing that was clean, well starched, and pressed. But she was embarrassed about her hair. It was brittle, broken, and falling out in spots.

Many black women had problems with their hair. These problems were caused by poor nutrition, poor health, or harsh shampoos or lotions. Sarah tried many hair products, but none worked.

This gave Sarah an idea. If she could come up with a hair treatment that would really work, she could start her own business. In 1905, Sarah came up with a mixture that would change her life. She later said, "God answered my prayer, for one night I had a dream. And in that dream a big black man appeared to me and told me what to mix up for my hair. I mixed it and put it on my scalp. In a few weeks my hair was coming in faster than it had ever fallen out. I made up my mind I would begin to sell it."

She decided to go west to start her new business. On July 21, 1905, she arrived in Denver, Colorado. She was 37 years old. Sarah rented a room in an attic. During the day she washed clothes. At night she worked on her products. After three months, she had developed three products that worked well on her own hair. They were Wonderful Hair Grower, Vegetable Shampoo, and Glossine. She also designed a steel comb with wide gaps between the teeth that would work well on thick, kinky hair.

Sarah McWilliams began selling her products door-to-door. Always, she would be beautifully groomed. She would give a free demonstration by washing the customer's hair with Vegetable Shampoo. Next, she put Wonderful Hair Grower on the customer's hair. She added Glossine, a light oil, to soften the hair. Last, she combed the hair with the steel comb, which had been heating on the stove. This process was later called the Walker Hair Care Method. It left the hair smooth and shiny.

Sarah began advertising in the local African-American newspaper. In her ads and on the labels of her products, Sarah used "before" and "after" pictures of herself. People began placing large orders through the mail.

On January 4, 1906, Sarah married C.J. Walker. She began calling herself Madam C.J. Walker. She thought this name would sound dignified and cultured. Also, the word *madam* sounded French, and Paris was the center of the fashion world at that time.

By this time, Madam C.J. Walker was earning $10 a week from her business. (The average black woman at the time earned $1.50 a week.) Sarah thought that women all over the country would buy her products if they knew about them. She made plans for an extended sales trip. Her husband laughed at her and told her she wouldn't make enough money to pay for the trip.

In September 1906, Madam C.J. Walker set out on a nine-state trip. Her daughter Lelia, who was then 21 and a college graduate, moved to Denver to supervise the mail-order business while Walker traveled. Madam Walker was doing more than just selling her product. She trained "Walker agents." These women would demonstrate and sell her products. By 1908 the income of her company had risen to $400 a month.

Madam Walker decided to move to Pittsburgh. In 1908, she and Lelia opened a beauty parlor there. They also started Lelia College, a training school for Walker agents. The college began graduating many "hair culturists." A correspondence course was also offered in the Walker Hair Care Method.

Most black women at this time worked hard at menial jobs for very little money. Madam C.J. Walker offered them a way to earn more money doing more rewarding work. Walker said, "I am proud that I have made it possible for many colored women to abandon the washtub for more pleasant and profitable occupations."

Two years later, in 1910, Madam Walker moved to Indianapolis, Indiana. (Lelia stayed in Pittsburgh to run the business there.) In Indianapolis, the business grew rapidly. Madam C.J. Walker started a beauty school, a laboratory for developing new products, and a factory. Nearly all the workers in her business were black women who lived nearby. Madam Walker's income rose to the astonishing figure of $1,000 a month. Her success led to problems with her marriage. In 1911 she and her husband divorced.

Madam C.J. Walker's products soon became controversial. Some black women accused her of trying to straighten their hair to make it look like a white woman's. Madam Walker argued that her purpose was to help black women have healthy hair.

In 1913, Lelia (who now called herself A'Lelia) adopted a daughter, Mae Bryant. As soon as Mae was old enough, Walker began teaching her about the business. The two traveled constantly, selling products and training new Walker agents. By this time, the Walker Company was grossing more than $100,000 a year. There were thousands of Walker agents around the country.

In 1913, A'Lelia opened a beauty salon in Harlem in New York City. Harlem was then the center of the town's black community. Famous composers, actors, poets, publishers, and businessmen settled there. Madam Walker decided to move there.

Madam C.J. Walker had developed the habit of sharing what she had while she was still a washerwoman. At that time she served as a member of the missionary society of her church. When she became wealthy, she began donating huge sums of money to various African-American causes. She gave $1,000 to the building fund for the Indianapolis YMCA. She also donated to Tuskegee Institute, Bethune-Cookman College, and a number of other African-American colleges. She was a big supporter of the NAACP. She helped many struggling artists and musicians get started. And she donated to churches and cultural groups.

Madam C.J. Walker was known for her loyalty to her own people. Madam Walker hired mostly African Americans, and she put her money into the black community. For example, when she built a housing project for black people in Indianapolis in 1916, the builders she hired were mostly black men. As she said, "My business is largely supported by my own people. So why shouldn't I spend my money so it will go back into colored homes?"

Madam C.J. Walker lived at a fast pace. For years, her doctor had asked her to slow down. She had developed life-threatening high blood pressure. Finally, in 1919, her doctor told her that she did not have long to live. Walker began making a list of groups she wanted remember in her will.

In May 1919, Madam C.J. Walker uttered her last words: "I want to live to help my race." On May 25, 1919, she died at the age of 51.

The Walker Company is still in business in Indianapolis today. On January 28, 1998, the U.S. Postal Service unveiled a commemorative stamp honoring Madam C.J. Walker. From washerwoman to millionaire, Madam C.J. Walker is a fine example of an entrepreneur. When she achieved wealth and status, she worked to help others of her race better themselves.

Remembering the Facts

1. Why was Sarah the only member of her family who was born free?

2. Why did Sarah not get an education as a child?

3. Why did Sarah decide to move to St. Louis after she was widowed?

4. Why did Sarah decide to make a hair treatment for African-Americans?

5. How did Sarah begin to sell her products?

6. Why did Sarah adopt the name Madam C.J. Walker?

7. What was Lelia College?

8. Why did the Walker Hair Care Method become controversial?

9. How did Madam Walker help thousands of black women?

10. What did Madam Walker do when she learned she was dying?

Understanding the Story

11. Madam C.J. Walker's business was an almost instant success. Why do you think that was so?

12. Why do you think it was difficult for black people to start businesses after the Civil War (and slavery) ended? What barriers do you think remained?

Getting the Main Idea

In what ways do you think Madam C.J. Walker gave black women an unequaled example of pride and self-determination?

Applying What You've Learned

Think of a product that would appeal to your peers. Design a label for its container. Write a few sentences telling how you would advertise the product to get your peers to try it.

James Rouse
Real Estate Developer

"Nobody really believes in the American city," James Rouse once said. "We have lived so long with old, worn-out ugly places that we have become (hardened) to their condition." But Rouse was a believer. Many people said America's inner cities were beyond hope. They wrung their hands about the crime and decay they saw. Rouse saw ways to make them vibrant, happy places full of people. Where some saw only run-down housing, he saw renovated affordable homes for the poor. James Rouse was a builder with a vision.

James Rouse

During Rouse's 50-year career in real estate, he changed the face of American cities. In the 1950's, he changed retailing forever by building the first shopping malls. In the 1960's, he built an entire town from scratch. In the 1970's, he revived the dying downtowns of many large cities. He spent the last two decades of his life working on decent housing for the urban poor. Indeed, Rouse brought change and hope to the 20th-century American city.

James W. Rouse was born in Easton, Maryland, on April 26, 1914. He was the fifth child of Willard and Lydia Rouse. Willard Rouse was a well-to-do canned foods broker. However, he wanted his children to grow up used to hard work.

James Rouse and his brother got up at 5:00 every morning to tend the family vegetable garden. They sold the vegetables to a local grocer. Later, James worked as a caddie for golfers. He also worked in a can factory.

James was a good student. He was president of both his class and the student council at Easton High School. He also belonged to the basketball and track teams.

James' comfortable life ended suddenly when he was 15. His mother died, followed a few months later by his father's death. His father left so many business debts that the Rouse children lost their family home.

James Rouse graduated from high school in 1930. He moved to Hawaii to live with his older sister. She helped him pay for a year at the University of Hawaii. The next year he won a scholarship to the University of Virginia, where he went for a year. But he had to drop out in 1933 because the Depression forced him to work full-time.

Rouse found a job parking cars in Baltimore, Maryland. He continued his studies at night. In 1937, he earned a law degree from the University of Maryland.

However, Rouse did not set up a law firm. He and a friend borrowed $20,000 from family and friends to set up a mortgage banking business. In 1939, he and his partner opened a firm that underwrote mortgages for one-family homes.

During World War II, Rouse was a lieutenant commander in the Navy Air Force Pacific fleet. At the end of the war, in 1945, he returned to Baltimore. He enlarged his company, underwriting apartment houses and shopping centers. By 1954, Rouse had bought out his partner, forming the James W. Rouse Company. By this time he was making large profits from his business. He began shifting his efforts into real estate development.

In the 1950's, suburbs began springing up around many large cities. Many people bought homes in the suburbs and drove into the city to work. Rows of small stores were strung out alongside the roads. Rouse thought these shopping strips were ugly and inefficient. He came up with the idea of putting a number of shops under one roof. People could park their cars in large lots. Then they could walk from store to store in air-conditioned or heated comfort. Rouse called this idea a "mall." Rouse built his first mall in 1958 in Glen Burnie, Maryland.

Rouse built more malls. But he soon tired of the lack of planning going into most cities and suburbs. His answer was to create an entire town from scratch. He named his town Columbia, Maryland. Rouse did not think of Columbia as a "utopia" (perfect place). Rather, he said it was just an effort to build a better city.

In the early 1960's, Rouse bought 14,000 acres of open land between Baltimore and Washington, D.C. He assembled a team of planners to discuss a model city. Rouse wanted to make it "a garden for the growing of people." He hoped to recapture the old sense of a village community in his town. He clustered nine villages around a downtown center. Each village had houses of different styles and a small shopping area. One-third of the "town" was left for playgrounds, parks, and conservation land. This included 78 miles of foot and bike paths and three lakes.

The first homes in Columbia went on the market in 1967. There were homes of all sizes and price ranges. People could buy single-family homes or rent apartments. The town was racially integrated. Rouse took pride in the way Columbia's population lived in harmony. Today, Columbia has a population of 84,000. Rouse himself lived the rest of his life there, in a modest home. He moved his company headquarters there as well.

In the 1970's and 1980's, Rouse turned his attention to America's decaying inner cities. Rouse had been interested in downtowns for years. In fact, he had coined the term "urban renewal" two decades earlier while working on a slum clearance project.

Rouse was asked by the city of Boston to help clean up its decaying downtown. Rouse took over a block of run-down, historic buildings that were more than 150 years old. He turned them into a lively complex of shops, restaurants, and offices. In 1976, the Faneuil Hall Marketplace opened. It now draws more than 15 million visitors a year.

Faneuil Hall Marketplace is the first example of what Rouse called the "festival marketplace." Rouse repeated this feat many times: Harborplace in Baltimore, South Street Seaport in Manhattan, Union Station in St. Louis, and the Grand Avenue in Milwaukee. Each festival marketplace is a delight. More than that, each spurred renewal of the surrounding downtown area.

In 1979, Rouse was 65 years old. He retired from his job as chief executive officer of the Rouse Company. (He continued part-time as chairman of the board.) But Rouse was not retiring from life. In fact, he was beginning what he would later call "the most important work of his life."

In 1981, Rouse unveiled the Enterprise Development Corporation. This group builds malls and downtown "festival market-places" across the country. The aim is to make profits, big profits. The profits go to fund the nonprofit Enterprise Foundation. Rouse said the goal of the Enterprise Development Corporation was "to build a development company that would make a gigantic fortune—not for the rich, but for the poor."

The Foundation provides advice and sometimes money and loans to neighborhood groups to help them reclaim decaying housing in poor areas. Rouse said, "The goal is to work from the bottom up in the neighborhoods. Not for us to do the housing, but for us to enable them (neighborhood groups, churches, civic organizations) to do the housing and deal with the lives of those in the housing."

When a neighborhood asks for help, the Enterprise Foundation sends a team to them. The team studies how existing buildings can be saved. It identifies which buildings should be torn down. Then the group shows the neighborhood how to finance, manage, and repair the buildings. It may also help convince businesses to get involved.

Rouse saw good housing as the best way to help the working poor help themselves. The program is not a give-away program. It is a way to give the urban poor a fresh start in life. Rouse said, "I feel that housing is not the answer to all the problems faced by the homeless and the poor. But it is the platform on which to build dignity, self-respect and hope in order that people can be helped with other problems they face. You've got to begin with housing—not stop with it—and work at the same time on better schools, better health care, jobs, teen programs."

The Foundation has worked with hundreds of local groups in cities around the country. By 1996, the Enterprise Foundation had helped to build more than 61,000 homes for the poor.

An example of a project helped by the Enterprise Foundation is Sandtown, a Baltimore neighborhood. Enterprise helped the neighborhood rebuild run-down houses. It also helped the people set up a job training program. It aided in efforts to reduce crime. It paved the way for improvements in neighborhood schools and health care.

Clearly, the Foundation was helping with much more than just housing. Rouse explained the reason in 1995. "It's my conviction that we cannot seriously improve the lives of the people at the bottom of our society today unless we do all these things at one time. And it is my conviction that it is far easier to do that all at one time than it is to approach the problems by the single shot approach."

James Rouse became more and more of an "urban evangelist." He preached the gospel of self-help urban renewal. Rouse believed that helping neighborhoods rebuild was morally right. He believed that he had a calling to do God's will on earth. One of the great commandments is to "love thy neighbor as thyself." Rouse sought to follow this commandment throughout his life.

In September 1995, President Clinton awarded James W. Rouse the Presidential Medal of Freedom. The medal is the nation's highest civilian honor. Donna Shalala, Secretary of Health and Human Services, called Rouse "a creative and passionate man who did more to revitalize American cities than anyone this century."

James W. Rouse died in 1996 at his home in his city of Columbia, Maryland. He was 81 years old. Rouse was a man of vision. He built towns, malls, and festival marketplaces. He used the profits from these ventures to help build housing for the poor. Rouse once said, "Profit should never be the primary motive for a developer. What should be important is to produce something of benefit to mankind. If that happens, then the profit will be there." James Rouse was an entrepreneur with a heart.

Remembering the Facts

1. How did the Rouse family lose their home in the late 1920's?

2. How did James Rouse earn his law degree?

3. What kind of business did Rouse set up after finishing law school?

4. Why were shopping malls an improvement over the shopping strips of the 1950's?

5. What feeling did Rouse hope to capture in his planned city of Columbia, Maryland?

6. What is a festival marketplace?

7. What is the purpose of the Enterprise Development Corporation?

8. What is the main goal of the Enterprise Foundation?

9. What award did Rouse receive in 1995?

10. Name three improvements the Enterprise Foundation made in the Sandtown neighborhood of Baltimore.

    (a)

    (b)

    (c)

Understanding the Story

11. Rouse's first idea for naming the Enterprise Foundation was the Robin Hood Foundation. Why do you think he thought that name would have been appropriate?

12. A writer for *Newsweek* said that Rouse had "the cold eye of an accountant, the touch of a Midas and the heart of a Sunday school teacher." What do you think he meant?

Getting the Main Idea

In 1981, James Rouse was chosen for the Hall of Fame for Business Leadership. Entrepreneurs who provide good role models for students are chosen for this group. Why do you think James Rouse was chosen for this honor?

Applying What You've Learned

Imagine that you've been asked to design a people-friendly shopping mall. Make a list of features you would include. Your aim is to make people feel happy and comfortable so they will enjoy spending time in the mall.

Mary Kay Ash
Cosmetics Entrepreneur

Mary Kay Ash created a huge cosmetics empire using three simple ideas: a small line of beauty products, a part-time female sales force, and prizes for top sellers. She turned a $5,000 investment into a multimillion dollar business. Today, Mary Kay, Inc., is among the best-selling brands of cosmetics in the United States. The company has 475,000 saleswomen in 25 countries.

Mary Kay (as she prefers to be called) was born Mary Kathlyn Wagner in Hot Wells, Texas, on May 12, 1918. When she was four years old, her father entered a tuberculosis sanatorium (hospital). He remained there for about four years. When he was able to come home, he was an invalid. He remained an invalid the rest of his life.

Mary Kay Ash

Mary Kay's mother was the sole support of her family. She managed a restaurant in Houston. She worked 14 hours a day. She was gone from 5:00 A.M. to 9:00 P.M. every day. This left seven-year-old Mary Kay to take care of her father. She would come home from second grade and clean the house and do her homework. She also had to cook dinner for her father. Her mother would give her help over the phone, always ending with the words: "Honey, you can do it." It was no wonder that Mary Kay came to believe that she could do anything!

Mary Kay credits her mother with encouraging her competitive spirit. Throughout her childhood, her mother would tell her,

"Anything anyone else can do, you can do better!" Mary Kay didn't want to let down her mother or herself. She worked hard to get straight A's. She tried to be the best at everything that she did. She sold the most Girl Scout cookies. She sold the most tickets to a dance. If she did not come out on top, her mother told her not to worry, but just to try harder next time. She finished high school in just three years.

When Mary Kay was 17 years old, she married a local singer named Ben Rogers. Rogers was a singer in a group called the "Hawaiian Strummers." After eight years of marriage, the couple divorced. Mary Kay was left alone to raise and support three children under the age of eight.

She looked for a job with flexible hours. She wanted to be home when her children needed her. She became a dealer for Stanley Home Products. She sold her wares door-to-door. She also hosted Stanley "parties." The "party" hostess would invite up to 25 people to her home for dessert and a sales pitch by the Stanley dealer.

Mary Kay liked selling. But what she really liked were the company contests. She set her sights on the annual "Queen of Sales" award. Borrowing $12 from a friend, she traveled to the company convention in Dallas. She asked that year's queen how she had done it. The next year Mary Kay won the prize! (It was a flashlight used to fish at night.) Years later, she remembered the thrill of winning that useless prize. When Mary Kay Cosmetics was formed, she used prizes (no flashlights) to spark sales with great success.

One evening in the early 1950's, Mary Kay was the dealer at a Stanley party in a poor part of Dallas. Twenty women were at the party. They ranged in age from 19 to 70. As Mary Kay showed her products, she noticed that every woman in the room had a smooth, unwrinkled face. After the party, she discovered the secret. The hostess was a beautician. She was using her guests as "guinea pigs" for a skin-care product she was working on.

The hostess's father had been a hide tanner. His hands were very soft and smooth, like a child's. He knew it must be because of the solution he used to cure hides. He tried the liquid on his face. When he died years later at 73, he had the face of a young man.

His daughter had seen her father's experiments. She took his solutions and worked with them herself. She wanted to develop creams and lotions that would be safe for women's skin. For 10 years, she had been selling them from her beauty shop. After the Stanley party that night, Mary Kay took some samples home. Soon she became a regular customer. When the beautician died in 1961, Mary Kay bought the formula from her heirs. She didn't want to be left without the creams.

Soon after this, Mary Kay left Stanley Home Products. She took a higher paying job at World Gift Company. This Dallas-based business sold home products. Mary Kay rose through the ranks. She became sales manager over a large territory. But she found that because she was a woman, she was paid a fraction of what men with the same job earned. She also learned that a woman could advance no farther in the company. These things seemed most unfair to her. Since she had now remarried and no longer had to work, she resigned in 1963.

After just six weeks at home, she was bored. She decided to write a book that would help other women in business. Mary Kay began by making two lists. The first included all the things that were wrong with companies run by males. The second told how the companies should be run to meet the needs of working women, especially working mothers. From these lists came her plan for her "dream company." It would be based on the Golden Rule: "Do unto others as you would have them do unto you."

Mary Kay soon realized that she already had a product to sell. It was the skin-care products she loved. Mary Kay put up her life savings of $5,000. She made plans for opening a small store from which the products could be sold. She had quantities of the creams and lotions made and developed packaging for them. She rented a small space in an office building.

Just a month before the store was to open, her husband died. Since he was to provide the financial expertise for the business, Mary Kay was unsure what to do. Her lawyer and her accountant strongly urged her to cut her losses and drop her plans. But her children rallied firmly behind her. They felt sure their mother could succeed in anything she tried.

So on September 13, 1963, Beauty by Mary Kay opened its first store. (Within two years the name changed to Mary Kay Cosmetics.) Mary Kay's 20-year-old son, Richard, was in charge of the store. Mary Kay set out to hire a sales force. She had decided to have women sell door-to-door as she had done years before. Her "consultants" would have no set hours. They would decide for themselves how hard and when they wanted to work. Most of her consultants were married or divorced mothers trying to earn a little extra money.

When Mary Kay planned her company, she wanted to sell a product so good that her sales force would believe in it whole-heartedly. She also wanted to create as easy a way as possible for women to buy cosmetics. She realized that most women did not know how to take care of their skin. So she invented the small beauty show. A consultant teaches a small group of five or six women about skin care. This way the consultant can answer every question. She can teach the women how to look their best.

The consultants use a low-key, educational approach. They do not sell the product; they instruct. Once a woman learns what products are best for her skin and how to use those products, she will usually continue to buy them. And in the rare case that a customer is dissatisfied, the company offers a money-back guarantee on all its products.

The cosmetics industry is extremely competitive. Giant companies like Avon and many department stores, have huge sales figures. But Mary Kay Cosmetics has topped them all. One reason is because she offers fewer products than her competitors. Therefore, her consultants can be experts in each product. Her smaller product list also means less inventory and lower overhead. Thus, she is able to sell her products for less money. Mary Kay's skin-care products make up fully half her cosmetic sales.

Another very important reason for her success is that Mary Kay knows how to motivate her sales force. Her consultants pay half of the retail price for the products. Then they resell them at full price, keeping the profit. They get bonuses for recruiting other women to be consultants. "Very Important Performers" can earn prizes, such as one of the company's famed pink Cadillacs. The top prize is a diamond bumblebee pin. The bee is a symbol of achievement to

Mary Kay. As she explains, "A bee shouldn't be able to fly. Its body is too heavy for its wings. But the bumblebee doesn't know this and it flies very well."

In 1987, Mary Kay became chairman emeritus (retired) of Mary Kay Inc. She continues to work to help other women achieve their full potential. Her company has been featured in *The 100 Best Companies to Work for in America.* Mary Kay has won many business awards and the prestigious Horatio Alger Award. (This award is given to select people who have built outstanding businesses from the ground up.)

Mary Kay has been active in raising funds for cancer research. In 1996, the Mary Kay Ash Charitable Foundation was established. It provides research funding for cancers affecting women. A cancer research wing at St. Paul Medical Center in Dallas was dedicated to Mary Kay. On the 30th anniversary of the company, in 1993, her employees presented her the Mary Kay/St. Paul Medical Center Mobile Cancer Screening Unit. Mary Kay has also worked to get laws passed in Texas to have insurance pay for cancer screening tests.

Mary Kay has written several books about how to manage people. Her latest book, *Mary Kay: You Can Have It All*, was published in 1995. It immediately became a best-seller. She has also written her autobiography: *Mary Kay: The Success Story of America's Most Dynamic Businesswoman.*

Mary Kay believes that the philosophy of a business determines its greatness. Mary Kay Cosmetics is based on three ideas. First is the Golden Rule. Second is living by the right priorities. The company motto is "God first, family second, career third." Third is the belief that everyone can be successful with enough praise and encouragement. "Praise people to success" is key to her style of management. Mary Kay believes that the success of her company depends on following these three beliefs. Mary Kay has left the running of her company to younger women. But she has left a legacy of caring, sharing, and giving that will live on.

Remembering the Facts

1. What three simple ideas are the basis of Mary Kay Cosmetics, Inc.?

    (a)

    (b)

    (c)

2. Why was Mary Kay's childhood challenging?

3. What company did Mary Kay work for when her children were small?

4. How did Mary Kay discover the products that later became the basis of her skin-care line?

5. Why did Mary Kay become frustrated working at World Gift Company?

6. What is the motto of Mary Kay Cosmetics, Inc.?

7. How does Mary Kay reward her "Very Important Performers"?

8. What type of sales approach is used by Mary Kay consultants?

9. Name one reason Mary Kay Cosmetics, Inc., has become the largest selling brand of skin care and cosmetics in the United States.

10. In what area has Mary Kay concentrated her charitable work?

Understanding the Story

11. Mary Kay credits her mother with much of her success. Why do you think her mother had such a strong influence on her?

12. Mary Kay Cosmetics, Inc., was featured in the book *The 100 Best Companies to Work for in America.* Why do you think the company was included in this book?

Getting the Main Idea

What do you think has been Mary Kay Ash's most important contribution to American business and society?

Applying What You've Learned

Imagine that you are the advertising director for Mary Kay Cosmetics, Inc. You have been asked to prepare an outline of a script for a television ad to sell Mary Kay products. Write a paragraph telling what approach you would take, using the Mary Kay sales philosophy.

John H. Johnson
Publisher

John H. Johnson's media empire includes Black Entertainment Television and the magazines *Ebony* and *Jet*. He also owns *Fashion Fair* cosmetics. In 1982, he was first named by *Forbes* magazine to its list of the 400 richest Americans. Johnson had come a long way from his humble beginnings.

Johnny Johnson was born in a tin-roofed shack three blocks from the Mississippi River in Arkansas City, Arkansas, on January 19, 1918. His mother, Gertrude, worked as a cook and cleaning woman. His father, Leroy Johnson, was a sawmill worker. He died in an accident when Johnny was eight.

John H. Johnson

One Sunday morning in April 1927, Johnny and his mother emerged from church. They saw swarms of people running up the streets in panic. Twenty-five miles up the Mississippi River, the levee had broken, causing one of the worst floods in American history. (A levee is a high ridge of land meant to keep a river from flooding.) Before it was over, 20 feet of water covered Arkansas City, forcing 800,000 people from their homes. The Johnsons were among the people who made it safely to the Arkansas City levee. They had to stay there for six weeks, until the water went down. Then they went home to find their house filled with mud. It was three blocks down the street from where it had stood. There was nothing to do but start over.

Gertrude had never gone past third grade, but she wanted a good education for her son. She sent him to the Arkansas City Colored School. It was a good school. But it went only through the eighth grade. There was no high school for African Americans in Arkansas City.

Gertrude decided that she and Johnny would take every extra job they could get until they had saved the money to move to Chicago where were black high schools. And in July 1933, they finally got there.

He later said, "When, late at night, we finally arrived at the Illinois Central Station…four blocks from what is now my corporate headquarters, I stood transfixed on the street. I had never seen so many black people before. I had never seen so many tall buildings and so much traffic."

By his senior year of high school, Johnny was editor of the school paper and sales manager for the school yearbook. He was president of the senior class. And he was to be the student speaker at the graduation ceremony. At this time his English teacher suggested that he change his name to John (his real name was Johnny) and choose a middle name. John chose the name Harold.

At a luncheon for black honor students, the speaker was Harry Pace. Pace was president of the largest African-American business in Chicago, Supreme Liberty Life Insurance Company. After the speech, John H. Johnson shook Pace's hand. Johnson told Pace about a partial scholarship he had received from the University of Chicago. He said that he still didn't have enough money to go. Pace suggested he go to college part-time and work for him part-time.

By 1940, Johnson was earning $100 a week. For the first time in his life, he could afford to date. In 1941, he married Eunice Walker.

Back at work, Johnson's job was to read newspapers and magazines and write for Pace a summary of the major happenings in the African-American world. At this time there was almost nothing in white newspapers about events in black communities, unless an African American committed a crime against a white. In fact, until the 1960's even marriages, deaths, and births of black people were omitted from white newspapers.

Johnson wanted to start a magazine similar to *Reader's Digest* that told stories about things important to black people. But no one Johnson talked to would give him a loan to get started.

He asked Pace if he could use the list of customers (all of whom were African American) of Supreme Liberty. In a letter, he asked each customer for $2 for a prepaid subscription to a new magazine to be called *Negro Digest*. This effort raised enough to publish the first issue on November 2, 1942.

In 1945, Johnson had an idea for a magazine with many pictures, similar to *Life* magazine. The magazine would do articles about black people of achievement, black society, and important events. The new magazine would be called *Ebony*.

From the start, *Ebony* had the largest circulation of any African-American magazine, as it does today. Even so, Johnson was losing money on the magazine. The cost of printing a quality magazine or newspaper is not met by sales alone. Advertising is needed to meet costs and provide a profit.

Johnson tried hard to get white companies to buy ads in his magazine. All refused. Finally, he had an idea. Nearly all African Americans owned radios. Zenith was the most popular brand. Johnson requested a meeting with the president of Zenith, Eugene McDonald. The meeting went so well that Zenith begin buying ads in *Ebony*. Other white companies followed suit.

It was not long before *Ebony* was outdoing *Negro Digest* in sales. It was hard for Johnson to give up publishing *Negro Digest*. But Johnson knew he must change with the times. Too often businesses fail because of what Johnson calls "the fatal disease, WWY—what worked yesterday."

In the 1960's, John H. Johnson became a national black leader. He worked for economic equality for African Americans in business. He tried to make companies realize that black people were consumers, too. By advertising in a black magazine, they would reach a whole new market.

Johnson's empire grew rapidly. In 1951, Johnson launched the magazine *Jet,* which became the largest African-American news magazine in the world. In 1973, Johnson bought a radio station. In 1974 he founded Fashion Fair Cosmetics, with makeup shades for black women. Also in 1974, he was named chairman of Supreme Liberty, the company which had given him his start.

Johnson became very popular as a speaker. Presidents invited him to the White House so they could learn more about African-American issues. Companies asked him to speak at meetings. He has served as a goodwill ambassador to several nations around the world.

In 1982, Johnson was listed by *Forbes* magazine as one of the 400 richest Americans. Today, Johnson Publishing Company is still the world's largest African-American-owned publishing company. In November 1995, the company launched *Ebony South Africa.* The company also owns Fashion Fair Cosmetics, Supreme Beauty Products, and Johnson Publishing Company Book Division.

Half a century after he founded his company, John H. Johnson remains publisher and chief executive officer. His daughter, Linda Johnson Rice, was named president and chief operating officer in the late 1980's. Johnson's wife, Eunice W. Johnson, serves as secretary-treasurer of the company. She is also the producer of EBONY Fashion Show, one of the world's largest traveling fashion shows. This show, started by the Johnsons in 1958, raises large sums of money for African-American charities.

When he was inducted into the Business Hall of Fame, Johnson spoke these words: "Long shots do come in . . . hard work, dedication and perseverance will overcome almost any prejudice and open almost any door. I believe that . . . what helps one group of Americans helps all Americans. And if my life has meaning . . . it is because millions of Americans, black and white, have proved through me that the Dream is still alive and well and working in America."

Remembering the Facts

1. How did Johnny and his mother survive the flood of 1927?

2. Why did Johnny and his mother move to Chicago in 1933?

3. Why was Johnson asked to be the student speaker at his high-school graduation?

4. How did Johnson get a job at Supreme Liberty Life Insurance Company after graduating from high school?

5. What did Johnson learn from his first job?

6. How did Johnson get the idea for *Negro Digest*?

7. How did he obtain the loan to publish the first issue?

8. Why did Johnson lose money on *Ebony* magazine at first?

9. Why did so many U.S. presidents and business leaders invite Johnson to speak to them?

10. As an African American, what did Johnson hope to achieve for his race?

Understanding the Story

11. Why do you think Johnson gives his mother credit for his success? Give examples from the story.

12. How do you think Johnson avoided catching what he called "the fatal disease in business: WWY"?

Getting the Main Idea

What do you think Johnson means by his statement: "Millions of Americans, black and white, have proved through me that the Dream is still alive and well and working in America"?

Applying What You've Learned

Imagine that you wanted to start a magazine to be sold in your school. Choose a name for your magazine. What kind of topics would you include? What local companies or groups might purchase advertising in your magazine? How would you distribute it to students? How much would you charge for a copy?

Fred Smith
Creator, Federal Express

For most of American industrial history, semiskilled workers labored in factories built close to the source of necessary raw materials. Trains and trucks brought the raw materials to the factories. Workers lived close to the factories, often in areas that were less than desirable.

In the 1960's, things began to change. The age of high-tech business was at hand. High-tech companies needed to attract highly trained scientists and technicians. To do this, they needed to locate in places these people wanted to live. Companies began to locate in widely scattered places across the country.

Fred Smith

This created a new problem. It was often necessary to deliver these high-tech products in a fast, dependable way. Fred Smith saw the need for a firm that could guarantee overnight delivery. Out of this need, Federal Express was born. Today, Federal Express delivers nearly a million packages a day. The company is worth $2 billion.

Fred Smith was born in Marks, Mississippi, to Frederick Smith and his wife, Sally. Fred Smith, Sr., was the son of a riverboat captain. He founded the Dixie Greyhound Bus Line and built it into one of the largest in the South. He also started Toddle House Restaurants, which became a national chain.

Fred Smith, Sr., died at 53, leaving his four-year-old son Fred fatherless. Fred was raised by his mother in Memphis. They did not lack for money. But Fred had another problem to overcome: a birth defect. A disorder of the bone sockets forced Fred to wear braces on his legs and use crutches. His mother did not want him to be weak. So, she encouraged him to take part in sports and other activities at school. By the time Fred entered high school, he had outgrown the disease and could walk normally.

Fred attended high school at Memphis University School. He became a good athlete. He especially enjoyed basketball and football. His peers voted him "Best All-Around Student."

Fred learned to fly a plane at 15. He earned his private pilot's license that same year. He also set up the Ardent Record Company with a group of friends. They set up a studio in the garage to record local rock and roll bands. The company was still in operation in the mid-1980's.

In 1962, Smith entered Yale University. He majored in political science and economics. He was not a very dedicated student. He was much more interested in his activities. Smith worked as a campus disc jockey. He enrolled in the Marine Corps Reserve Officers Training Corps (ROTC). His interest in flying grew. He revived the Yale Flying Club, which had been started after World War I by Juan Trippe (who later founded Pan Am airlines).

For his economics class, Smith finally got an assignment that excited him. He was asked to write a paper about an idea for a new business. Smith did an analysis of the air freight industry. He found that few packages were being sent directly to their destination by the carrier service. Instead, they were "hippety-hopping around the country from city to city and from airline to airline before reaching their destination." This was a big waste of money and time. If someone was sending a package airmail or special delivery, they wanted it to arrive quickly. Smith thought there would be a market for a company that could deliver packages in one day.

Fred Smith's professor was not impressed with Smith's logic. He argued that Smith's company would need its own fleet of airplanes. That would be expensive. He said Smith could never raise enough money to start the business. And he said that there would be too much competition from existing airlines, to say nothing of the U.S. Postal Service. Fred Smith got a *C* on his paper!

At the time, the paper seemed unimportant to Fred Smith. It was 1966, and he was graduating from college. He was commissioned a second lieutenant in the Marine Corps. He did two tours of duty in the Vietnam War. During his second tour, he went to flight school. He flew more than 200 ground-support missions. Smith rose to the rank of captain. He won the Silver Star, the Bronze Star, and two Purple Hearts.

Smith returned to the United States in 1969. He decided to start a business based on his love of flying. Smith used part of a trust fund left to him by his father to buy Arkansas Aviation Sales. The company repaired and serviced airplanes. It had been losing money every year. Smith changed things at Arkansas Aviation. The company began buying and selling used jets. Within two years it was making a healthy profit.

But Fred Smith found the business boring. He kept thinking about his old idea of delivering small packages overnight. He wondered who was really right: he or the Yale professor? He hired two consulting firms to study the idea some more.

At that time, package delivery was done by two giants: the U.S. Postal Service and UPS (United Parcel Service). Two smaller services were Emory Air Freight and Flying Tiger. These latter two provided services a little like what Smith had in mind. But Smith's consultants showed there was a lot of room for improvement.

The consultants found that many customers were not satisfied with the existing freight services. They could not count on deliveries being on time. The consultants agreed with Smith. There was a market for a company that could pick up small packages and deliver them on time without mistakes. Customers were willing to pay higher prices to get assured deliveries. Fred Smith had been right.

Fred Smith decided to go ahead with his idea. In June 1971, Federal Express Corporation was incorporated. For the next two years, Fred Smith worked on his business plan.

The plan centered on what he called a "hub and spoke" system. All packages would be flown at night, when 90 percent of commercial airliners were on the ground. This meant no waiting for take-offs and landings. All packages would be flown to a central location to be sorted. Next they would be rerouted to their destinations. Delivery would take place in the morning. Smith limited the size of packages to 75 pounds to make loading and unloading easier.

Smith chose Memphis, Tennessee, as the hub of his system. Memphis was his hometown. It had good weather conditions year round. And it had ample facilities to handle the traffic.

Now all Smith had to do was raise the money he needed to buy the planes. It wasn't long before he figured out why no one had tried the idea before. It would require an enormous amount of capital to get his plan in operation. And it wasn't easy to convince investors that his plan would work.

Fred Smith put up $8 million in family funds. He convinced private investors to put up another $40 million. Several banks added another $40 million. In all, Smith raised $90 million. It was the largest single venture capital startup in American history!

Smith ordered 33 small twin-engine jets. He also ordered a fleet of small delivery trucks. Federal Express would offer three services. It offered overnight delivery. Second-day delivery was available at a reduced rate. A "Courier Pak" delivered anything that would fit into a special envelope for $5.

Federal Express began operation on April 17, 1973. It started with service to 22 cities. The first night only 186 packages were shipped. This was a real blow to Fred Smith. And things did not get better very quickly. In its first two years of operation, Federal Express lost $30 million.

But Fred Smith would not give up. He sold nearly everything he had to be able to pay his employees. Smith's dedication inspired his employees. Delivery people often left their watches as security when there was no money to buy gas for their truck. Employees hid company trucks and planes when sheriffs came to repossess them. One employee later recalled: "This company should have died five or six times in its first three or four years. But Fred refused to give up. With sheer courage, he pulled off a miracle. That's the only way to express what he did."

In July 1975, Federal Express had its first profitable month. In 1977, airlines were deregulated. Now Federal Express could use larger planes to carry more packages to bigger cities. And it could fly smaller jets almost anywhere. That year, Federal Express made a profit of $20 million. In April 1978, a million shares of FedEx stock were offered at $3 a share. Two years later, the shares were selling for $24. Fred Smith and his backers had finally made a fortune.

There were three reasons for the success of Federal Express. The first was Fred Smith's drive and persistence. He also had the ability to motivate his employees to work hard for him.

The second reason Federal Express succeeded was because it was so well organized. Six nights a week, FedEx planes zoom into Memphis. There they are unloaded. Packages are sorted and rerouted. The employees are well-paid, part-time workers. Many are college students. They work between 11 P.M. and 3 A.M. Electronic scanners read the bar codes on the packages. This tells the ZIP code of the destination. In the early hours of the morning, the packages are shipped back out on the same fleet of planes. When they arrive at the airport of destination, they are sorted again. They are then placed in a delivery truck for final delivery that morning. It works! Federal Express has an outstanding record of delivering packages on time.

The third key to the success of Federal Express was advertising. The company's distinctive color scheme is easily recognizable. Every ad stressed the slogan: "absolutely, positively overnight." They stressed the unreliability of their competitors.

By 1984, Federal Express was flying high. It continued its rapid growth through the 1980's. In 1989, Smith purchased one of his rival companies, the Flying Tiger. This allowed Federal Express to expand its international routes. Today, Federal Express offers next-day service to many countries around the world. It offers service to the farthest corners of the earth within 48 hours.

Today, Fred Smith remains the head of Federal Express. There are 130,000 FedEx employees around the globe. In 1997, the company's net income was $361 million. Fred Smith's schoolboy scheme has made him rich. And his career with Federal Express is being examined in business schools as a prime example of entrepreneurship in our time!

Remembering the Facts

1. What two problems did Fred Smith have to overcome as a child?

   (a)

   (b)

2. What special hobby did Fred Smith take up at age 15?

3. Give two reasons Smith's Yale professor did not like his idea for a business specializing in rapid package delivery?

   (a)

   (b)

4. What business did Smith take over when he returned from the Vietnam War?

5. How does the "hub and spoke" system work?

6. How did Smith raise the capital to start Federal Express?

7. What is FedEx's slogan?

8. What did airline deregulation mean to Federal Express?

9. Where is the company headquarters of Federal Express?

10. How are the packages sorted?

Understanding the Story

11. Why do you think advertising played such a large role in the success of Federal Express?

12. Why do you think people are often willing to pay premium prices to use the services of Federal Express?

Getting the Main Idea

The story of Fred Smith and Federal Express is used as an outstanding example of entrepreneurship in business schools. Why do you think Smith is a good role model for business students?

Applying What You've Learned

Make a list of times when it would be vital to have a package delivered "absolutely, positively overnight."

Robert Swanson
Biotechnology Scientist

The Industrial Revolution took place from about 1750 to 1850. It brought the world into the machine age. In the late 1960's, a second "industrial revolution" began. This was the coming of the information age, based on computers.

Around 1975, another "revolution" was beginning. Scientists had just learned how to clone genes. Robert Swanson thought that this technique could be used to make medicines. Swanson knew nothing about cloning. But within a few short years, he would form a company that would dominate the emerging field of biotechnology. He was about to create a new industry.

Robert Swanson

Robert A. Swanson was born on November 29, 1947, in Brooklyn, New York. As a boy, Robert was excited by the space race between the United States and Russia. He decided he wanted to become a chemist. He and his parents studied the idea. They decided that MIT (Massachusetts Institute of Technology) was the best college for him to study chemistry.

MIT was difficult to get into. Swanson worked hard all the way through high school so that his grades would be good enough. In 1965, he graduated tenth in his class of 1,200 students at Hialeah High School. When he was accepted at MIT, the whole family was proud. No one in the Swanson family had ever finished college.

The Swansons took a risk in sending Robert to MIT. He said, "We only had enough money for my first year. If I didn't get a scholarship after that, it was back to a state school. That was another of my family's values. We said, 'Let's go for it.'" Luckily, Swanson did earn that necessary scholarship the next year.

Swanson worked hard at MIT. He earned his bachelor's degree in chemistry in just three years. Then he entered MIT's Sloan School of Management. At Sloan, he took a course about venture capital. (Venture capital is money raised to start a new company.) He found the idea of building his own company exciting.

Swanson received a master's degree in business in 1970. He took a job with Citibank in New York. Three years later, Citibank sent him to San Francisco. There he opened a venture capital branch of the bank. He enjoyed working for Citibank. But soon he felt the need for a change.

He accepted a job with Kleiner & Perkins, an important venture capital firm in the area. It was an unusual job. He was asked to think about new places the firm could invest other people's money. The firm hoped he would come up with great ideas so investors would make lots of money.

Swanson left Kleiner & Perkins after a year. He had become interested in the infant science of genetic engineering. In 1973, two scientists named Herbert Boyer and Stanley Cohen figured out how to take genetic material from two different organisms and piece them together to make one new gene. Then they got the gene to reproduce itself. This reproduction is called cloning.

Since Swanson had a good background in chemistry, he was able to read and understand scientific articles explaining the developments about cloning. He talked to experts in the field. He read everything he could get his hands on. Swanson said, "The more I heard about this new technology, the more excited I got. I knew, I was completely convinced, that this was going to be great."

Swanson thought cloning could be made into a business. He saw it could be used to create new medicines. He discussed his idea with scientists in the field. They all thought that commercial uses for cloning would take at least 10 years.

In 1975, Swanson set up an interview with Herbert Boyer at the University of California at San Francisco. Boyer was an overworked and underfunded biochemist. He really didn't want to talk to Swanson. Finally, he agreed to a 15-minute interview late on a Friday afternoon. Boyer was entranced by Swanson's vision for commercial uses for cloning. They talked far into the night. Boyer was convinced that Swanson had a workable idea.

Soon, Swanson had convinced his former boss, Thomas Perkins, to give him start-up money for the new business. In April 1976, Genentech, Inc., was formed. The name is an abbreviation of "genetic engineering technology." Swanson would run the company. He hired Boyer to oversee the labs. Swanson, a secretary, and nine scientists set up shop in a South San Francisco warehouse.

The group decided to work first to make synthetic insulin. Insulin is normally made by the pancreas. It helps keep the body's blood sugar at the right level. If the body fails to make enough insulin, diabetes results. People with diabetes often take insulin to regulate their blood sugar level. At one time, insulin was obtained from the pancreas of sheep. It was hard to get. By cloning the gene for human insulin, a plentiful supply would be available. Genentech achieved this goal in 1978. In 1982, synthetic human insulin became the first drug made by cloning to reach the market.

On October 14, 1980, Genentech became the first biotech firm to go public. It was perhaps the most anticipated stock offering in history. It took exactly one minute for all the shares of stock to be sold. Then the shares began to be traded on the stock market. The initial price of one share was $35. In less than one hour, the stock price was up to $88 a share. Robert Swanson made half a billion dollars in just one day!

Genentech has made many more miracle drugs. And Genentech scientists continue to work on cures for cancer, arthritis, and AIDS.

The list of its products reads like a history of biotechnology. In 1984, Genentech came up with a blood-clotting factor. This drug has helped people with hemophilia lead more normal lives.

The year 1987 saw the debut of Activase. It is an anti-heart attack drug. Activase works by dissolving blood clots in the arteries. It has been very successful in preventing a second heart attack.

Genentech has been very successful. Swanson's management style is a big part of that success. To succeed, Genentech had to attract excellent scientists. To do that, Swanson offered them something they could get nowhere else. Genentech gave its scientists the funds they needed to do their work. They no longer had to worry about competing for grants. It allowed them flexible working hours and freedom to work on their ideas. Genentech provided the latest equipment and support services. It also allowed scientists to publish their work in scientific journals. All of this produced a good working environment. Employees were judged by the quality of their work and ideas. The people who made the discoveries got the credit for their work.

Swanson served as director and CEO of Genentech until 1990. Now retired from the company, he is a major patron of the arts. He has served on the board of the San Francisco Ballet and the San Francisco Museum of Art. He has also endowed a "chair" in the Department of Biology at MIT. The Robert A. Swanson Professorship is awarded to a young professor who shows great promise for the future.

Genentech has made a real contribution to the quality of American life. It was the first company to make medicines using the technology of gene cloning. The company shot into the ranks of America's *Fortune 500* companies faster than any other start-up in history. Genentech's scientists have been second to none in using gene cloning to produce medicines to improve life for millions of people around the world.

Remembering the Facts

1. What new field developed around 1975?

2. How did Robert Swanson decide to go to MIT?

3. What two degrees did Swanson earn at MIT?

4. What kind of work did Swanson do for Kleiner & Perkins?

5. What technique did Boyer and Cohen discover in 1973?

6. What is the name "Genentech" short for?

7. How did Swanson get the start-up money for Genentech?

8. What was the first product made by Genentech?

9. What does Activase do?

10. How was Genentech a good working environment for scientists?

Understanding the Story

11. Why do you think people were so excited when Genentech stock first went on the market?

12. Why do you think Robert Swanson and Herbert Boyer made such an outstanding leadership team for Genentech?

Getting the Main Idea

Why do you think Swanson's background put him in such a good position to see the commercial possibilities of cloning medicines?

Applying What You've Learned

Imagine that you are a young scientist working for Genentech. Write a paragraph telling what you imagine your work would be like.

Ben Cohen and Jerry Greenfield
Ice-Cream Makers

In 1978, Ben Cohen and Jerry Greenfield opened a homemade ice-cream shop in an old, run-down gas station in Burlington, Vermont. Ben & Jerry's is now a $160-million international company. Ben and Jerry make great ice cream! But they also use their business as a tool for social change. They call their method "values-led business." Their commitment to social values has paid off big in profits and loyalty of their customers and employees.

Ben Cohen and Jerry Greenfield were born in 1951 in Brooklyn, New York. The two boys met in junior high school after their families had moved to Merrick, New York.

Ben Cohen (top) and Jerry Greenfield

Ben and Jerry were the two slowest, fattest kids in the seventh grade gym class. On the day they met, the class was running laps on the school track. The coach yelled, "Cohen! Greenfield! If you can't do the mile in under seven minutes, you're going to have to do it again." Ben answered, "But, Coach, if we can't do the mile in under seven minutes the first time, how are we going to do it in under seven minutes the second time?" From that day on, they knew they would be friends!

All through junior high and high school, the two were best friends. During the summers, they worked for Ben's father, sorting direct-mail ads by ZIP code.

Another thing the friends had in common was the love of food, especially ice cream. Ben had inherited his love of ice cream from his father, who often ate a half-gallon of ice cream after dinner.

In their senior year, Ben got a job driving an ice-cream truck. The happiness on the children's faces when they took their first taste of the ice-cream treats made a strong impression on Ben.

After high school, Ben and Jerry headed to college. Ben applied to only one college: Colgate University. He chose Colgate because the catalog said there were fireplaces in each dorm. Ben was not a serious student. After taking classes at several colleges, he dropped out for good in 1972.

Jerry applied to several schools but was accepted only by Oberlin. His plan was to become a doctor. But when he graduated, he could not find a medical school that would admit him.

Jerry gave up his plan of becoming a doctor and headed back to New York. There he got together with Ben, who had spent the previous few years doing odd jobs. The two decided to go into business together.

Since both loved to eat, a food business seemed like a good choice. They wanted to start their business in a small town. And they wanted to make something they liked to eat. Ice cream!

Neither of them knew anything about making ice cream. So they signed up for a correspondence course from Penn State. It cost $5, and they were broke. So they sent in one fee and split the course. After passing the exam, they figured they knew enough to get started.

The next question was where to put their store. They decided on Burlington, Vermont. It had a young population with lots of college kids. And it did not have an ice-cream parlor!

Ben and Jerry moved to Burlington. They found an old abandoned gas station downtown. They signed a one-year lease and began to work on their ice-cream recipes. It was the winter of 1977–78. There was no heat in the gas station. There were six inches of ice on the floor. They could see daylight through holes in the roof. Ben and Jerry lived on saltines (three boxes for a dollar) and sardines (three cans for a dollar). When they needed a break from working, they went down the street to the bus station, where they could use the bathroom and warm up.

Their first few tries at making ice cream yielded mixed results. Jerry later said an early batch of rum raisin was so badly mixed that it "stretched and bounced." But by summer they were turning out delicious batches of ice cream mixed in a 4 ½-gallon freezer. When they ran out, they hung a "No ice cream" sign in the window.

People loved their ice cream. But they loved coming to Ben & Jerry's even when the ice cream was sold out. Customers drank the fresh-squeezed lemonade and listened to the piano player. Or they just came in to hang out.

Ben and Jerry were what many people in the 1960's and 70's called "hippies." Hippies believed that people should think more about peace and love and less about making money. Jerry later said, "When we grew up, it wasn't cool to be businessmen." So, their goal was to make people happy with their ice cream, not to become rich.

At the end of the first year, the business wasn't making any money. But Ben and Jerry had promised each other that if they made it through the first year, they would celebrate by giving away ice cream. On May 5, 1979, they began the anniversary celebration they still carry on today: Free Cone Day. Every year on this day, all Ben & Jerry's stores give away free ice cream cones all day.

For the next three years, Ben & Jerry's sales increased. But each year they failed to make a profit. To keep their product "the people's ice cream," they had kept their prices too low. It was clear that they had a choice: raise prices or go out of business. So, they raised their prices.

Ben and Jerry began expanding their business. In 1980, they bought an ice-cream factory and started selling their ice cream in local stores. The ice cream was a big hit. The public liked their unusual flavors, such as Chunky Monkey®, Cherry Garcia®, and Rainforest Crunch®. Time magazine called it the "best ice cream in the world." Today, Ben & Jerry's Ice Cream is sold in nearly every state. By April 1997, there were 168 Ben & Jerry's Scoop Shops.

Every carton lid shows a picture of the two partners enjoying their product.

When they started their business, Ben and Jerry had two goals. First, they believed that work should be fun. "If it isn't fun, why do it?" became their motto. Ben and Jerry knew how to have fun. They held parties and funny contests for their employees. In 1983, they created the world's largest sundae, earning a spot in the Guinness Book of World Records. The sundae weighed 27,102 pounds and was covered with 1,400 pounds of syrup! In 1988, Ben created his "Joy Gang." Its purpose was to bring joy and laughter to employees of Ben & Jerry's. They wanted their workers to feel as though they were part of a family.

Ben & Jerry's second goal was to help the community. The company donates 7.5 percent of its profits to community groups. Many of these groups focus on helping needy children. The Ben and Jerry Foundation helps groups that clean up the environment, teach people job skills, and treat drug-addicted mothers.

Ben and Jerry work by a business model called "values-based" business. Values-based business is based on the idea that business has a responsibility to the people who support it. In a larger sense, it has a responsibility to society as a whole. Values-based business means more than just giving money to good causes. (Many profit-oriented businesses do make charitable contributions.) It means business decisions are based on social values, not profit. Socially beneficial actions must be a part of the day-to-day operation of the company. In other words, the mission and operations of the company must center on the values the company leaders think are important. This is different from a traditional business model that makes decisions based on profit first.

Ben's and Jerry's values lead what they do. Their values center on helping other people and working to save the environment. So, every decision they make must work toward these goals. For example, before they buy milk from a dairy, they make sure that the dairy treats its employees fairly and doesn't pollute the environment. They buy nuts from the rain forests to discourage the cutting down of trees there. They treat their own employees well, providing good benefits and a pleasant working place.

As Ben and Jerry say in their book, *Ben and Jerry's Double Dip:* "Business has now become the most powerful force in society. We cannot solve social problems unless business accepts a leadership role. That in turn requires the business to act in the interests of the common good.... Business is just a tool. It can be used to improve the quality of life in general or just to maximize profits."

As Ben and Jerry have shown, a values-led business can still be highly profitable. Many customers are loyal to a company if they believe in the company's values. Employees will work harder for a company that cares about their welfare. When consumers, employees, and investors feel loyalty to a company, profits will increase.

Ben and Jerry also feel that there's a spiritual aspect to business which is usually overlooked. Love, kindness, and caring need to be a part of every aspect of our lives, including the workplace.

Over the years a lot of people have questioned whether values-based business could work. At first, Ben & Jerry's was criticized by the media, by Wall Street, and by other business leaders. But it has come to earn the respect of those same critics. For Ben Cohen and Jerry Greenfield have proven that a socially responsible business can indeed work!

In 1988, Ben and Jerry were named Small Business Persons of the Year. The award was presented by President Ronald Reagan. As he presented the award, Reagan repeated a phrase often included in business textbooks: "The business of America is business." Ben and Jerry would put a new twist on that old saying. Their version is, "The business of business is America." As Ben and Jerry have shown, what's good for America is also good for business.

Remembering the Facts

1. Where did Ben and Jerry open their first store?

2. What is values-led business?

3. How did Ben and Jerry learn to make ice cream?

4. What tradition did Ben and Jerry start on the anniversary of their first year in business?

5. Why didn't Ben and Jerry make a profit during their first three years in business?

6. What is the motto of Ben & Jerry's?

7. What is the name of the book Ben and Jerry wrote to explain their business philosophy?

8. What is the most powerful force in society, according to Ben and Jerry?

9. Why can a values-led business be especially profitable?

10. What award did Ben and Jerry receive from President Reagan in 1988?

Understanding the Story

11. Ben and Jerry say, "Values are either a forethought or an afterthought. There's no middle ground." What do you think they mean by this?

12. How do you think you, as a consumer, can influence businesses?

Getting the Main Idea

In what ways do you think that Ben & Jerry's Ice Cream symbolizes a new kind of company?

Applying What You've Learned

Imagine that you are starting a business to manufacture a food product. What things could you do to make sure that your business will be values led?

Oprah Winfrey
TV Talk Show Host

Oprah Winfrey is the world's richest entertainer. She became the first woman to top the *Forbes* list of highest paid performers. Oprah was born to a single mother who abandoned her soon after birth. She was raised in poverty by her grandmother in rural Mississippi. Bright and ambitious, Oprah Winfrey was determined to have a better life than she saw on grandmother Hattie Mae's pig farm. Her journey to wealth, power, and success is an amazing story.

Oprah Winfrey

Oprah Gail Winfrey was born on January 29, 1954, on a small farm in Kosciusko, Mississippi. Her father, Vernon Winfrey, was a soldier on leave from a nearby army base when he met her mother, 18-year-old Vernita Lee. They were never married. Soon after Oprah was born, Vernita left for Milwaukee to find work. She left her baby to be raised by her mother, Hattie Mae Lee.

Oprah and Hattie Mae worked hard on the farm all week. On Sunday they attended the Buffalo United Methodist Church. Oprah remembers the Sunday schedule: "You did Sunday school. You did the morning services which started at 11:00 and didn't end until 2:30. You had dinner on the grounds in front of the church. Then you'd go back in for the 4:00 service." Reading the Bible and prayer remain a daily part of Oprah's life today.

When the chores were done, Hattie Mae taught Oprah her letters and numbers. By the time she was three years old, the little girl could read and write. She also loved to memorize and recite poems. Whenever a program was planned at school or church, Oprah would be asked to recite. By the time she was four years old, everyone in town knew Oprah was gifted. The women of the church called her "the little speaker." Oprah could hardly wait for the person in charge of the program to announce, "Little Miss Winfrey will now recite!" Oprah loved being on stage, always feeling perfectly at ease. Her "broadcasting career" had already begun!

When Oprah was six, her mother asked her to come live with her in Milwaukee. Vernita worked hard for long hours. So Oprah was often left at home alone or in the care of a neighbor. She did not understand why her mother paid so little attention to her. She began to get in trouble. When she was nine years old, she was raped by a cousin who was supposed to be baby-sitting her. Later, she was repeatedly sexually abused by her uncle.

Oprah kept this abuse to herself. But she became more and more angry. She kept getting in trouble. Vernita could not make her behave. By the time she was 14, Oprah was running wild. She gave birth to a premature baby, who died. Finally, Vernita decided to send Oprah to a juvenile detention home. Luckily for Oprah, there was no space in the home. She was sent to live in Nashville with her father. He had married, owned a barbershop, and served on the Nashville city council.

Vernon Winfrey set up strict rules for his daughter. He knew she was gifted and that she could succeed if she worked at it. He made her choose five words from the dictionary every day to learn. Then he quizzed her on the words at dinner. She also had to read one book a week and write a report for him. Oprah did not mind this because she loved to read.

Oprah began getting her life together. At Nashville East High School she was a good student. Oprah signed up for a class in public speaking and the drama club. When she heard about a speech contest held by the local Elks Club, Oprah entered. She won first prize, a scholarship to African-American Tennessee State University.

The summer before she started college, Oprah was hired to read the news and weather on WVOL radio. She continued this work while she was attending college as a speech and drama major. The pay was good, and she loved the work. In 1972 she won the "Miss Black Nashville" and "Miss Black Tennessee" contests. She came in first in the talent and personality sections.

In 1973, a local television station offered her a job. Oprah quit her radio job. She became a television anchorwoman at the age of 19. She was earning $15,000 a year as the first female, and first African-American, newscaster in Nashville.

In 1976, just two months before she was to graduate, she was offered a full-time job as a reporter for a television station in Baltimore, Maryland. It was too good to pass up. But soon she found she was not cut out to be a reporter. A reporter should report the news, leaving emotions and personal opinions out of it. Oprah was unable to do this. She was always more concerned for the people involved than for the news itself. Her boss fired her. Then he gave her another job. She would cohost a morning talk show called "People Are Talking." After just one day on the show, Oprah knew this job was right for her. She was able to talk easily with all kinds of people. She could say what she thought and learn what the audience thought. Oprah stayed at this job for seven years.

But Oprah wanted more. She had always wanted to live in Chicago. So, in 1984 she sent tapes of her show to a faltering talk show called A.M. *Chicago*. She was hired and quickly made the show the hottest show in town. The station expanded the show to an hour. In 1985, the show was renamed "The Oprah Winfrey Show." People loved the show. By 1986, it was being shown nationally. Oprah became the first African-American woman to host a national show aimed at an audience of all races.

Soon the show had twice as many viewers as any other daytime talk show. In 1987 the show won three daytime Emmy awards. Many other Emmys have followed. In 1988 Oprah bought her show from the network. She was the first woman to own and produce her own talk show. The deal was made by HARPO Productions, Inc., the production company she had formed in 1986. (Read the word HARPO backwards to see where she got the name.) She also owns her own TV and film studio.

"The Oprah Winfrey Show" has a new theme every day. It may be a celebrity interview. It may be a discussion on AIDS, drug abuse, or racism. Experts in the field and people who have experiences relating to the topic are invited on the show as guests. Oprah leads a discussion of the day's topic, including questions and comments from the audience. This is basically the format used by all talk show hosts. But Oprah's show is different.

It is different because of her ability to connect with people. She has been very open on the air about her own life and her many problems growing up. She is so open and friendly that people feel at ease talking about themselves. Oprah seems to sense what the audience most wants to ask a guest, and she does not hesitate to ask it. People seem to be so charmed by her that they reveal their innermost secrets. Yet, however shocking the revelation, Oprah always seems to understand. She is everyone's best friend.

One of the goals of the show is to help other people. Oprah knows that people watch the show and learn that they are not alone in their problems. People learn that other people have overcome their problems, giving them hope of doing the same.

Despite her fame, it bothered Oprah that she had not finished her college degree. Eleven years after she left college, she returned to finish her degree. When she graduated, she was also the speaker at the graduation ceremony. She announced that she would send money to Tennessee State University to fund 10 scholarships a year in the name of her father, Vernon Winfrey.

Oprah believes that education is the key to success. As she says, "Education is important because it is a way out. You get to read about, if not see, a sort of place where life can be better. Your belief combined with your willingness to fulfill your dreams is what makes success possible."

In 1985, Oprah's career expanded into a new area: movies. She played the role of Sophia in *The Color Purple*. She was nominated for an Academy Award for her first movie performance. Her second movie role was as Mrs. Thomas in the movie based on Richard Wright's book *Native Son*. And she is starring in a HARPO-produced movie version of Toni Morrison's novel *Beloved*.

Many of the films made by HARPO are based on important works of African-American literature. "Brewster Place" was a 1990 miniseries based on Gloria Naylor's book, *The Women of Brewster Place.* The series shows everyday life in a black community. *Beloved* by Toni Morrison describes a woman's escape from slavery. *Kaffir Boy* tells the story of Mark Mathabane, who grew up in South Africa under apartheid. Zora Neale Hurston's book *Their Eyes Were Watching God* tells of a black girl's coming of age. With all these films, Oprah seeks to educate, as well as entertain, people. "Good film is one of the best ways to raise consciousness," she once said.

In 1993, HARPO made a movie called *There Are No Children Here.* It is the story of two boys growing up in a housing project. The movie was shot in the project where the story took place. After the filming was over, Oprah set up a tutoring program and a scholarship program for the children living there.

Oprah is involved with many charities. She gave $1 million to Morehouse College, an African-American college in Atlanta. She contributes to the Chicago Academy of the Performing Arts. She gives money to help battered women and victims of AIDS.

In 1997, television's richest woman got a lot richer. Oprah agreed to host the show for two more years for $130 million. She has also agreed to make six television movies for ABC.

Television talk shows have come and gone. But "The Oprah Winfrey Show" is the longest running syndicated hit on television. Oprah tries to choose worthwhile topics to do on her show. She hopes to help other people realize their full potential, as she is seeking to reach hers.

Oprah is a black woman in a field dominated by white men. She has made it to the top with her talent and determination. She is one of America's best talk-show hosts, actresses, and businesswomen. As Oprah says, "I try to be the best at what I do. I always have since the first grade. When you are the best, it is hard for people to keep you down.... Watch out! I'm going to fly!" Most people would agree, she already has!

Remembering the Facts

1. Name two ways Oprah's grandmother gave her a firm foundation for life.

2. When did it become clear to everyone in her hometown that Oprah was gifted?

3. What saved Oprah from being sent to a juvenile home?

4. How did Vernon Winfrey get his daughter under control?

5. How did Oprah get the money to attend college?

6. Why was Oprah not cut out to be a news reporter?

7. How did Oprah get her start as a talk show host?

8. For what movie was Oprah nominated for an Academy Award?

9. What type of movies are made by HARPO?

10. Name two charities supported by Oprah.

Understanding the Story

11. When Oprah was hired by the television station in Baltimore, she knew she would be their "token" African American (the only black person they hired). Why do you think she took the job anyway?

12. What do you think are the pros and cons of talk shows in American culture?

Getting the Main Idea

Oprah says, "Good film is one of the best ways to raise consciousness." What do you think she means? Do you think she succeeds in doing this in her movies and with her talk show?

Applying What You've Learned

Imagine that you are going to produce a week-long series of talk shows for your high school class. Make a list of the five topics you would include. The topics should be interesting and important to your peers. There should also be sufficient material available to fill an hour each.

Bill Gates
Founder of Microsoft

In the late 1960's, computers were an infant technology. Computer programs were simple, requiring information to be punched in on cards and fed to the computer. The computers themselves were huge. A single computer could fill a whole room. They were also very expensive. Only the government, very large companies, or universities could afford to buy a computer.

Bill Gates

Bill Gates was a teenager during those years. But already he had a dream. He dreamed of "a world in which machines would do all the boring parts of work and people would be free to be creative and productive." He dreamed of a world with "a computer on every desk and in every home, all running (my) software." Today, Bill Gates is watching some of his dream becoming reality. *People Weekly* says of Gates: "Gates is to software what Edison was to the light bulb—part inventor, part entrepreneur, part salesman and full-time genius."

Bill Gates was born in Seattle, Washington, on October 28, 1955. His father, William Gates, was a prominent lawyer. His mother, Mary Gates, was active in civic affairs. Bill had two sisters.

Bill was skinny and small for his age. Not only that, he was the youngest person in his class. But Bill Gates was smart. By the time he was nine years old, he had read every volume in the *World Book Encyclopedia*.

Bill attended public school until sixth grade. He was often bored in class. So, his parents sent him to Lakeside School, an expensive private school. They hoped he would get the extra attention he needed there.

In 1968, Bill was in the eighth grade. That was the year he got his first taste of computers. Like most schools, Lakeside School could not afford a computer. Instead, it bought an ASR-33 Teletype machine. This machine could communicate with a real computer in a large company downtown. It was not long before Bill was spending every possible minute with the ASR-33. He read everything he could get his hands on. Soon he was writing programs using a language called BASIC to use through the teletype machine. His first was a tic-tac-toe program.

Another student who was interested in computers was Paul Allen. Paul was two years older than Bill. Paul and Bill joined with two other Lakeside boys to form the Lakeside Programmers Group. Bill Gates was chosen as president of the group because he was the only one who liked to read business magazines.

When Bill was just 14, he and Paul got their first jobs with computers. A local business had just purchased a computer on unusual terms. As long as there were "bugs" in the system, they did not have to pay for the computer. The business hired the boys to find those bugs. Every day after school, the two boys hopped on their bicycles and rode to work. They found so many bugs that the business never had to pay for the computer!

The next year, the two boys were hired by a government defense contractor. Lakeside School gave Gates a semester off from school to work there full-time on an important project. (Paul Allen had already graduated.) This experience gave them the chance to sharpen their programming skills.

The boys decided they were ready to start their own company. It would be called Traf-O-Data. Cities often needed to collect data on traffic patterns. The data would tell whether a traffic light was needed at an intersection. A rubber hose was placed across a road. When a car crossed the hose, the time was recorded on a tape. The two boys built a computer to analyze the data. Many cities hired Traf-O-Data. But once it became known that the company was run by teenagers, business fell off.

That didn't matter because Bill Gates was ready to go to college. Since he had made a perfect score on the math section of the SAT, every college in the country wanted him. Gates chose Harvard. There, in 1973, he began studying law. He also spent a lot of time at Aiken Hall, the school's computer center.

Gates also enjoyed reading electronics magazines. The January 1975 issue of *Popular Electronics* did a cover story on a computer called the MITS Altair 8800. The story called the machine "the first personal computer." It could be built from a kit. There was no software for the computer, so it would not actually do anything. Yet thousands of hobbyists paid $397 for the Altair 8800.

Bill Gates and Paul Allen saw that a language was needed for the Altair. They decided to adapt BASIC for it. BASIC was a simple language known to many computer hobbyists. Gates and Allen called Ed Roberts of MITS. They told him they had written a version of BASIC for the Altair. Roberts was very interested and asked to see the software. The boys said they could deliver it in four weeks. There was only one problem. There was no program! Gates and Allen began writing it fast. For eight weeks, they worked day and night. Gates skipped all his classes at Harvard as the deadline neared, then passed.

When the program was finished, Paul Allen flew to Albuquerque to present the program to MITS. He was chosen to do the presentation because he looked older than Gates. It was a tense time. The boys had not had a machine to test the program on. They had written the program using a manual that described the Altair. But when Allen loaded the program, it worked perfectly. The Altair was now a working computer. Ed Roberts was impressed. He offered Paul Allen a job at MITS as software director.

Bill Gates finished his second year at Harvard. That summer, he joined Paul Allen in Albuquerque. They knew it was time for them to form their own company. As Gates later wrote in his autobiography, "When I was 19, I caught sight of the future and based my career on what I saw. I turned out to have been right."

The new company was Microsoft. The name came from the words *microcomputer* and *software*. Microsoft was set up as a partnership between Gates and Allen.

In 1976, Paul Allen left MITS to work full-time for Microsoft. In 1977, Bill Gates took a leave of absence from Harvard, never to return to college. At the end of that year, the company moved to Seattle, Washington. They worked with other companies such as Apple Computers, Commodore Computers, and the Tandy Corporation. By 1980, Microsoft had 80 employees and $8 million in revenues. But that was nothing compared to what happened next.

In July 1980, Gates received a call from IBM, the computer giant. They wanted to meet with him that very day. Gates ran out immediately to buy a tie. IBM employees always wore blue suits and starched white shirts to work—hence the name "Big Blue." Gates decided his usual working uniform of jeans and a T-shirt was not right for the occasion.

IBM's project was top secret. Before IBM would reveal the nature of the project, they asked Gates to sign a nondisclosure agreement. That meant he agreed not to discuss the project with anyone else. IBM was developing a secret microcomputer. They wanted Microsoft to write an operating system for it. They also wanted BASIC software written for the computer. And they wanted both projects done within a year.

In November 1980, a deal was drawn up. IBM would provide Microsoft with models of its secret new computer. Microsoft would develop the operating system and software. Bill Gates insisted that Microsoft would retain ownership of any software it developed for IBM. For the right to use the software, IBM would pay royalties (a percentage of the profits) for each IBM computer sold with Gates' operating system, MS-DOS. That would later prove to be a costly mistake for IBM.

In August 1981, IBM introduced the IBM PC. It quickly became the standard for the computer industry. Other computer companies wanted their computers to work on a compatible system. So, they also used Microsoft's operating system, MS-DOS. It was not long until Microsoft was supplying the operating systems for 90 percent of the IBM PC's (and compatible machines) sold in the United States. By 1984 Microsoft's profits were over $15 million.

In 1982, Paul Allen became ill with cancer and was forced to leave Microsoft. Gates now had to run the company himself. (Later,

Allen beat his cancer. He returned to the Board of Directors of Microsoft.)

The year 1983 was a good one for Microsoft. Gates continued to develop new products that he hoped would become industry standards. Microsoft Windows was developed. In April 1983, Microsoft introduced the Microsoft Mouse. Then in September, a word-processing program, Word for MS-DOS, came out. It became one of the most popular word-processing programs in the world.

On March 13, 1986, Microsoft went public. Now the public could buy shares (stock) of Microsoft. The sale of these shares gave Gates more money to expand the company. Shares were sold for $21 each. By the end of the first day, Gates had raised $61 million for Microsoft. Gates had become a multimillionaire overnight. And he was just 30 years old.

By March 1987, the price of a share of Microsoft had reached $90.75. Since Gates owned 45 percent of the shares, his wealth also climbed. At the age of 31, Bill Gates found himself a billionaire.

Many Microsoft employees shared in Microsoft's success. When the company was young, Gates had paid his programmers low salaries plus shares of stock. When the company went public, these employees made fortunes on their gamble with the company. Today, there are more than 3,000 "Microsoft millionaires." Paul Allen and one other executive became billionaires.

Gates kept building on his successes. Microsoft began flooding the market with new products. These new software programs sold at computer stores for between $50 and $500. Yet they cost Microsoft only about $10 to manufacture. Clearly, the profit margin was great.

Microsoft continued to grow. In 1986, it moved to a new 270-acre site in Redmond, Washington. The grounds are called the Corporate Campus. The average employee on the Campus is 34 years old. Two-thirds of the workers are male. Dress is casual, usually jeans and a T-shirt. Employees work long hours, up to 80 hours a week. Yet the climate is friendly and high spirited. There are lots of parties for employees and free membership in a nearby health club. All the employees know that however late they work, Bill Gates will probably be there working when they go home.

On January 1, 1994, Bill Gates married Melinda French. She worked in the Microsoft marketing department. The couple had a baby girl in 1996. His competitors hope family life will slow Gates down.

Today, Bill Gates is the wealthiest man in the United States. In 1997, *Forbes* magazine listed his net worth as about $40 billion, and climbing.

You may wonder what he does with all that money. He keeps expanding his business into new areas such as cable TV and the Internet. He built a $50 million house near Microsoft headquarters. He collects art and famous manuscripts.

Gates also donates money to charity. He and his wife set up a $200,000,000 foundation. Its purpose will be to put computers in public libraries that serve underprivileged neighborhoods. Gates donated $12 million to the University of Washington for bioengineering research. He gave the same university another $10 million for an endowment in his mother's name. He gave $6 million to Stanford University for a computer science center.

Some people have criticized Gates for not giving away more of his money. In a January 30, 1998, television interview with Barbara Walters, Gates explained his views on wealth. He said, "I will have the privilege and responsibility of taking that wealth and giving it away in a way that helps out people who haven't had the same opportunities." He went on to say "the money will be given away in my lifetime."

Gates feels he will have years to give his money away. He is still putting his energy into building his company. He shares many of his ideas for the future in his autobiography, *The Road Ahead.* In it he talks about some of his ideas for new uses for the computer. He describes a "pocket computer" and a "wallet PC." He also talks about the many new software projects underway at Microsoft.

Bill Gates' dream of "a computer on every desk and in every home" is rapidly coming true. Who knows what the future will hold in the world of Microsoft and Bill Gates?

Remembering the Facts

1. What kind of machine did Lakeside School buy in 1968 that started Gates' interest in computers?

2. What was Traf-O-Data?

3. What program did Gates and Allen write for the Altair 8800?

4. Why did Gates drop out of Harvard?

5. Where did the name Microsoft come from?

6. What two things did Microsoft develop for IBM in 1980?

7. How did IBM end up paying Microsoft huge royalties?

8. How did Gates become a multimillionaire overnight in 1986?

9. Why did Gates become a billionaire in 1987?

10. Name three software products made by Microsoft today.

Understanding the Story

11. *Forbes* magazine says Gates' net worth doubled in one year (1996 to 1997) from $20 billion to $40 billion. Why do you think his wealth keeps growing at such an enormous rate?

12. What factors in Gates' personality do you think have contributed most to his success?

Getting the Main Idea

People Weekly said "Gates is to software what Edison was to the light bulb." What do you think they meant?

Applying What You've Learned

Imagine that you are a software engineer for Microsoft. Write a paragraph describing a computer program that you would like to see developed. Explain what things the program would do. Choose a name for it.

Jerry Yang
Developer, Yahoo!

Ice dancing. The Mayan Indians. The saber tooth tiger. Life on Mars. No matter what the subject, it probably can be found on the Internet's World Wide Web.

The problem can be finding what you want among the millions of pages on the Web. That was something that Jerry Yang and David Filo realized "way back" in 1994. The two graduate students loved "surfing the net." There was lots of great stuff there. The problem was that if you didn't know the address of the site you wanted, it wouldn't be easy to find it. It was like looking for a book in a large library with books shelved in random order.

Jerry Yang

Yang and Filo made a list of their own favorite Web sites. They began to organize their list into categories. Friends asked to use their list. So, they set up a site to share their list.

Soon, the project was taking all their time. Yang and Filo were in typical start-up mode. They worked 20 hours a day. They slept in their office. The list grew rapidly. As other people discovered their site and loved it, Yang and Filo became more and more excited about it. There was only one difference between them and most new entrepreneurs. They weren't making any money. They were just having a blast untangling the Web.

Yang and Filo added a search engine. They named their service "Yahoo!" (for *Yet Another Hierarchical Officious Oracle*). Yahoo! quickly joined the most popular services on the Web. By the end of

1994, Yahoo! was being accessed a million times a day. By 1997, their site was getting a billion hits per month. What began as a late-night hobby now makes millions of dollars from ads each month. Today, Yahoo! shows no signs of slowing down.

In 1968, Jerry Yang was born Chih-Yuan Yang in Taiwan. His father died when Jerry was only two. His mother was a professor of English and drama. When Jerry was 10, he, Ken, and his mother came to the United States. They settled in San Jose, California. Jerry's mother had a sister living there. She thought it would be a good place for her boys to grow up.

Jerry and Ken Yang started school. The only word of English Jerry knew on that first day of school was "shoe." He quickly learned English and excelled in school. He was admitted to Stanford University. He majored in electrical engineering.

Jerry completed both his bachelor's and master's degrees in just four years. He interviewed for a few jobs at this point. But he quickly decided he "wasn't ready to work yet. I had the degree of a master's but I didn't have the experience or the maturity. I was barely 21. So I looked for ways to stay in school." Yang decided to enter a Ph.D. program in electrical engineering at Stanford.

David Filo had grown up in Louisiana. He had a bachelor's degree in computer engineering from Tulane. Filo entered Stanford's Ph.D. program in electrical engineering. There he met Jerry Yang. The two students shared a tiny office in a university trailer.

Officially, Yang and Filo were working on their Ph.D. dissertations. But their faculty advisor was taking a year's sabbatical in Europe. The two got sidetracked. They began spending all their time surfing the Web. In early 1994 Yang and Filo put "David and Jerry's Guide to the World Wide Web" on-line. Soon this directory, renamed Yahoo!, edged graduate school out of their lives.

The reason Yahoo! became popular so quickly is that it is easy to use. It is organized into hierarchies. On the top level are 14 broad categories. Subjects include business and economy, entertainment, health, and so forth. Beneath each category is a group of subcategories. Each of these in turn leads to more precise categories. Today, there are over 400,000 Web sites cataloged, with new sites being added weekly.

Users who don't want to surf down through the categories can type the subject they want into a search window. A list of sites then comes up.

Yahoo! is different from other search engines. All of its thousands of categories were designed by people, not computers. Other search engines take key words and conduct a rote search for pages that contain them. Thus, a large number of links are listed, most of them irrelevant. Yahoo!'s links are set up using human logic. This is hard work. But it yields better results for the user.

From its beginning, Yahoo! was free to its users. Even though it was wildly popular, Yang and Filo had not made a penny from it. But they knew that there must be a way to do so. At the end of 1994, Yang asked a college friend to write a business plan for them.

When the plan was finished, Yang and Filo invited Mike Moritz of Sequoia Capital to discuss it with them. (Sequoia was a venture capital fund that had backed other computer companies.) In *Architects of the Web*, Moritz describes this meeting. Yang and Filo were "sitting in this cube (the trailer) with the shades drawn tight, the Sun servers (computers) generating a huge amount of heat, the answering machine going on and off every couple of minutes, golf clubs stashed against the walls, pizza cartons on the floor, and unwashed clothes strewn around. It was every mother's idea of the bedroom she wished her sons never had."

Even so, Yang and Filo somehow impressed Moritz. In April 1995, he agreed to back them with $1 million. Other investors signed on. In exchange for cash, Yang and Filo gave the investors 12 percent of the company.

At that same time, America Online (AOL) was the largest on-line service. It needed a search engine. So, they offered to buy Yahoo! Yang and Filo would work for them. Yang and Filo thought about the offer. It would have meant a lot of money. But they liked working for themselves. Therefore, they turned it down. (AOL later bought a search engine called WebCrawler.)

Soon they were contacted by Netscape. Like AOL, Netscape wanted to buy their service. They turned down this offer too. But Netscape did not buy another search engine. Instead, it linked its

"Internet Directory" button directly to the Yahoo! site in 1995. This made it easy for the millions of people then discovering the Web to also discover Yahoo!

Yahoo! was growing rapidly. Yang and Filo knew they needed help from someone who knew business. They hired Tim Koogle to manage the company. Filo remained in charge of the engineering team. Yang worked on business relations and outside relations.

The first order of business for the new team was to figure out how to make some money. They quickly ruled out charging people for their search service. In August 1995, they decided to charge advertisers $20,000 for every 1 million times Yahoo! customers viewed their ad. It worked! Many companies began advertising on Yahoo! First quarter ad sales in 1997 were nearly $10 million.

Yahoo! continued adding to its service. In August 1995, Yahoo! added a news service from Reuters. In December 1995, a weather service was added. Stock quotes became available in 1996.

In December 1995, Netscape decided that its "Internet Directory" button would now point to one of Yahoo!'s rivals, Excite. The button had been pointing to Yahoo! for nearly a year. It had brought a good percentage of Yahoo!'s hits. No one was sure what would happen when the change was made.

In January 1996, they found out. They lost less than 10 percent of their traffic. It was clear Yahoo! could stand on its own.

On April 12, 1996, Yahoo! went public. Its shares were priced at $13. Trading of the shares was wild. By the end of the day, they were going for $33.

The story of Jerry Yang and David Filo is legend in Internet lore. The two have been on countless TV shows and magazine covers. Yahoo! has millions of loyal customers who love the company's idealism and "trailer to riches" story.

Today, Yahoo! is working to build its image. The first Yahoo! book, *Yahoo! Unplugged,* has done well. A quarterly magazine and CD-ROM package, called *Yahoo! Internet Life,* has appeared on newsstands. Yahoo! is also advertising its service on TV and in magazines. Its slogan is "Do You Yahoo!?"

A new product called "My Yahoo!" hopes to keep Yahoo! users loyal. My Yahoo! users enter their interests into a system that makes personalized pages for them. Users can visit their personal pages to find the things that interest them bundled in one place and easy to find. For example, people interested in sports scores, weather reports, and news headlines can access all these things from "My Yahoo!"

In April 1996, the first international Yahoo! was launched in Japan. It has been followed by editions in other countries. And there is even a "Yahooligans!" for the 8- to 14-year-old set.

It seems there is no end to the possibilities for the Internet. It seems to be moving far too quickly to guess what might come next! Jerry Yang loves every minute of his work with Yahoo! In *Architects of the Web,* he said, "I love what I'm doing. I don't even see it as a job."

Jerry compares the newness of all this to "being dropped off a helicopter, and you're the first guy skiing down this hill. You don't know where the tree is, you don't know where the cliff is, but it's a great feeling....We have nothing to lose. We started this with nothing, and I can honestly say I don't mind if we went back to nothing, because I had a great time."

But financial success has brought a few changes to the "Chief Yahoo." He no longer lives in the trailer, working day and night. He and his fiancee Akiko have bought a house. He works only from 7 a.m. to 10 p.m. these days. And he even takes off one day on the weekends.

It's too early to know the future of Yahoo! It isn't easy keeping it fresh, lively, and at the forefront of Web servers. Every day new companies pop onto the scene. But Jerry Yang is committed for the long haul. "We believe the Internet can change lives," says Yang. It certainly changed his!

Remembering the Facts

1. Where was Jerry Yang born?

2. Why was Yang at a disadvantage when he started school?

3. How did Yang and David Filo meet?

4. Why did Yang and Filo have so much "free time" to surf the Web when they were graduate students?

5. How is Yahoo! organized?

6. Why did Yang and Filo make no money from Yahoo! in 1994?

7. Why did Yang and Filo hire Tim Koogle in 1995?

8. Name two features that were part of Yahoo!'s new look in 1995.

   a.

   b.

9. What event took place on April 12, 1996?

10. What is "My Yahoo!"?

Understanding the Story

11. Why do you think Yahoo! is popular among people in their teens and twenties?

12. Why do you think Yang and Filo did not want to work for a large company, such as America Online or Netscape, even if it meant more money?

Getting the Main Idea

Why do you think Jerry Yang says of Yahoo!, "I don't even see it as a job"?

Applying What You've Learned

Imagine that you have the service "My Yahoo!" Make a list of the types of Web sites you would include on your Web page. Examples might include these: news, weather, sports scores.

Vocabulary

Frederic Tudor, the Ice King
- judge advocate
- exclusive
- parallel
- consumption
- practicality
- preservation
- grooves
- abundant
- speculation
- hazardous
- brochure
- inventory
- insulation
- cultivation

Biddy Mason, Philanthropist
- midwife
- constitution
- financial
- obituary
- custody
- homestead
- Mormon
- precedent
- grueling
- commercial

Andrew Carnegie, Steel Industrialist
- bobbin
- innovation
- financial
- competition
- accounting
- dispose
- homestead
- immigrant
- malleable
- precedent
- phenomenal
- Bessemer process
- commercial
- reinvest

Montgomery Ward, Catalog Sales Wizard
- exotic
- rural
- bankruptcy
- hamlet
- parcel
- retail
- apprentice
- shoddy
- reorganization
- catered
- progressive
- environ-
  mentalist

King Gillette, Inventor of the Safety Razor
- disposable
- utopia
- obsessed
- stropping
- patent
- vise
- honing
- corporation
- socialism
- crimped
- lather
- straight razor

Henry Ford, Automotive Pioneer
- assembly line
- futuristic
- philanthropic
- mechanical
- reliable
- pacifist
- devastated
- multitude
- luxurious
- threshing
- conveyor belt
- asset

Madam C.J. Walker, Hair-Care Innovator

- lye
- culturists
- brittle
- controversial
- menial
- cultural
- self-determination
- commemorative

James Rouse, Real Estate Developer

- retailing
- integrated
- caddie
- conviction
- underwrite
- evangelist
- mortgage
- motive

Mary Kay Ash, Cosmetics Entrepreneur

- cosmetics
- competitive
- motivate
- tuberculosis
- beautician
- retail
- sanatorium
- expertise
- potential
- invalid
- consultants
- priorities

John H. Johnson, Publisher

- media
- scarce
- registration
- consumers
- emerged
- corporate
- partial
- perseverance
- levee
- transfixed
- subscription
- advantage

Fred Smith, Creator, Federal Express

- high tech
- repossess
- destination
- incorporated
- deregulation
- bone sockets
- commercial
- international
- venture capital
- consulting firm
- entrepreneurship

Robert Swanson, Biotechnology Scientist

- biotechnology
- clone
- synthetic
- genetic
- hemophilia
- hepatitis
- diabetes
- insulin
- biochemist
- patron

Ben and Jerry, Ice-Cream Makers

- commitment
- socially
- lease
- beneficial
- environment
- responsible
- correspondence

Oprah Winfrey, TV Talk Show Host

- ambitious
- Emmy award
- scholarship
- personality
- celebrity
- apartheid
- faltering
- revelation
- syndicated
- anchorwoman
- consciousness

Bill Gates, Founder of Microsoft

- software
- revenue
- underprivileged
- teletype
- compatible
- royalties
- internet
- microcomputer
- nondisclosure

Jerry Yang, Developer, Yahoo!

- World Wide Web
- sabbatical
- quarterly
- internet
- accessed
- search engine
- hierarchy
- site
- irrelevant

Answers

FREDERIC TUDOR, THE ICE KING

Remembering the Facts

1. The spice business
2. He and his brother were joking about ways to make money.
3. Martinique
4. His inventory of ice melted, and he was left $4,000 in debt.
5. He packed it in sawdust and then insulated it with hay. It was stored in an icehouse.
6. It enabled him to quickly cut more evenly shaped chunks of ice which were easier to store and to ship.
7. Boston was losing much of its shipping business to New York before Tudor began shipping huge amounts of ice.
8. It is using artificial ponds to form ice quickly.
9. They were shallow, so they would freeze over quickly. Ice could be removed and then the ponds reflooded.
10. Well insulated in the holds of fast clipper ships, it could travel to China.

Understanding the Story

Answers will vary.

11. People enjoyed different types of food, such as ice cream and cold drinks. They had a larger variety of food because foods could be kept fresh longer. Ice could help them cool off in hot weather.

12. There are fewer instances of food poisoning. People get a more balanced diet. Doctors can use ice to treat patients. Ice can help bring down a fever.

Getting the Main Idea

Answers will vary. He created a demand for a product there had previously been no demand for. He solved many problems to ship the ice over long distances. His business was unprofitable for many years, but he never lost sight of his dream.

Applying What You've Learned

Answers will vary. Following are examples: No ice cream or cold drinks, fruit only when it is in season, less selection of meats

BIDDY MASON, PHILANTHROPIST

Remembering the Facts

1. She helped the household servants and midwife.
2. He was a Mormon and wanted to help build Salt Lake City.
3. Any three: organized the camp, herded animals, prepared meals, midwife, took care of her children
4. He learned that California law forbade slavery, and he feared losing his slaves.
5. She went to court against Smith and won.
6. She worked as a nurse and midwife for a doctor.
7. She bought land that was well located and grew much more valuable.
8. Mason never turned away a person who was in need.
9. First African Methodist Episcopal Church
10. A memorial in the form of a time line wall at the Broadway Spring Center

Understanding the Story

Answers will vary.

11. Mason had been taught to obey her master. Also, if she had lost the suit, he might have taken revenge on her and her daughters.
12. She was very thrifty. She saved until she could buy a good parcel of land. When it appreciated, she sold a small part and bought more land. By reinvesting her money wisely, she made it grow.

Getting the Main Idea

Answers will vary.

She helped people of all races. She delivered thousands of babies for families all over the area. She visited the sick and those in jail.

Applying What You've Learned

Scenes might include the following: her birthplace as a slave; working as a slave as a little girl; learning midwifery; walking to Utah, then California, behind the wagons; herding cows, oxen, and mules; winning her freedom in court; buying her first piece of land; delivering babies; walking around Los Angeles with her black medical bag; and a line of people outside her home on Spring Street.

ANDREW CARNEGIE, STEEL INDUSTRIALIST

Remembering the Facts

1. He could not compete with factories that made linen faster and cheaper.
2. He was a bobbin boy.
3. Children could be made to work long hours for low pay in unsafe or undesirable working conditions.
4. He gained access to businesses, offices, and homes he would not otherwise have seen and met influential people.
5. He was already making more money with his assorted business ventures, and he wanted to be his own boss.
6. He saw that most of his other ventures depended on iron, so he decided to concentrate his efforts in one field.
7. Steel was stronger and more malleable than iron. When a process was discovered that allowed it to be made cheaply, Carnegie knew steel was the wave of the future.
8. The Industrial Revolution was producing machines that were made of steel. Railroads were being built.
9. He said that a man who died with his fortune intact was disgraced. He felt that money should be used to better mankind.
10. He knew he would not be able to give away all his money in his lifetime. The foundation would spend just the interest it earned so that his donations would continue indefinitely.

Understanding the Story

Answers will vary.

11. Cost accounting allowed Carnegie to see exactly how efficient each step of the process was and where improvements needed to be made.

12. *Agree:* The money could be used to help the needy. Too much money given to children or family could make them "soft" and take away their drive to work.

    Disagree: A person's family and friends deserve to get all the money as an inheritance.

Getting the Main Idea

The American Dream is the idea that anyone of any background can succeed with hard work. Carnegie's story is not only a classic rags to riches story but a story of a generous man who expressed through his actions his love for humanity.

Applying What You've Learned

Any reasonable causes are acceptable, excluding family, friends, and the student.

MONTGOMERY WARD, CATALOG SALES WIZARD

Remembering the Facts

1. He worked in a general store and then later as a traveling salesman.
2. Any three: poor selection, high prices, shoddy merchandise, inconvenient to travel to the store
3. The Chicago fire of 1871 destroyed it.
4. One sheet of paper listing 163 items for low prices.
5. He offered them a guarantee of "satisfaction or your money back."
6. The Grange, a farmers' organization
7. It brought mail service directly to farmers' homes.
8. Sears, Roebuck and Co.
9. Catalog sales dropped when farmers could drive to stores.
10. Rudolph was invented by a Ward's advertising man.

Understanding the Story

Answers will vary.

11. They had few books, little entertainment, and no access to stores. It seemed like magic to get a book in the mail "to wish on."

12. When people could drive to stores and shop, they no longer needed Ward's catalog. Catalogs today, in general, sell specialty or hard-to-find items more than basic-needs items.

Getting the Main Idea

Ward found a need and filled it. Catalog sales and the money-back guarantee were innovations whose time had come. The catalog opened up a whole new kind of merchandising.

Applying What You've Learned

A school catalog could include faculty, students, courses taught, rules, clubs, grading system, a school calendar, etc.

KING GILLETTE, INVENTOR OF THE SAFETY RAZOR

Remembering the Facts

1. As one of history's great social reformers
2. She wrote a cookbook with recipes and household hints.
3. Gillette was forced to quit school and work.
4. Working and living conditions for workers were poor. Cities were full of crime and poverty.
5. *The Human Drift*
6. He wanted to promote his ideas for social reform.
7. Any two: The blade had to be sharpened. It took a lot of time. Men often cut themselves. Going to a barber was time consuming and expensive.
8. How to mass-produce it
9. World War I
10. Arizona, Theodore Roosevelt

Understanding the Story

Answers will vary.

11. By earning money with his business, he hoped to promote his socialist ideals. In the end, he hoped his ideals would prevail.

12. Yes. There are many problems to overcome in designing a product for the mass market.

Getting the Main Idea

Answers will vary.

Many of his ideas were not very practical. They often fail to take into account basic human nature. Also, such radical changes would not be easy to achieve.

Applying What You've Learned

The campaign could involve rebates on razors, a contest, coupons, giving away a poster of King Gillette, etc.

HENRY FORD, AUTOMOTIVE PIONEER

Remembering the Facts

1. She was the only member of his family who believed in him.
2. He wanted Henry to become a farmer.
3. Any two: watch repair, Michigan Car Company, Flower Brothers, Detroit Drydock, repairing farm machinery, demonstrating Westinghouse engines
4. Any two: bicycle wheels with rubber tires, two speeds, four horsepower, no brakes, no reverse gear
5. Edison praised him, saying that he had the right idea.
6. He began building and driving race cars, attracting the attention of wealthy men when he won.
7. It was sturdy and inexpensive. The design was simple, so it was easy to run and to care for.
8. The workers began to feel like robots, doing the same task over and over at a rapid pace.
9. Other manufacturers were making larger, luxurious cars.
10. He wanted to own the sources of all the products that he used to make and distribute his cars.

Understanding the Story

Answers will vary.

11. The assembly-line process made it possible to make the cars very efficiently. Buying the sources of his raw materials created further savings.
12. To Henry Ford's father, security was a job on the land. He did not see why Henry would want to live or work in the city.

Getting the Main Idea

The pace of life quickened. A highway system was developed. The economy of the nation changed from one that was largely based on farming to one based on factories.

Applying What You've Learned

A color scheme, sound system, soft drink holders, etc.

MADAM C.J. WALKER, HAIR-CARE INNOVATOR

Remembering the Facts

1. The others were born before the end of the Civil War.
2. There were few schools for black people, and the children were needed to work in the fields.
3. She heard the wages were higher there. Also, there was a large black community.
4. Her own hair was brittle, damaged, and falling out. She knew many other black women had the same problem.
5. She went door-to-door, giving free demonstrations.
6. She married C.J. Walker. The term *madam* sounded dignified and French.
7. A school that trained Walker agents to be hair culturists.
8. Some African Americans said she was trying to make black hair like the hair of white women.
9. She hired them and enabled them to make a better living. She also gave them a sense of pride in themselves.
10. She listed where she wanted her money given.

Understanding the Story

Answers will vary.

11. She had a product that filled an important need.
12. Most African Americans were uneducated and penniless. White banks would not lend to them or buy their products or services.

Getting the Main Idea

Madam C.J. Walker showed these women an alternative to menial labor. She had come from a background as poor as any of them, yet she was able to be highly successful.

Applying What You've Learned

Answers will vary.

Accept any reasonable product and label. Advertising techniques could include posters, radio or TV spots, ads in the school newspaper, in-home product parties, etc.

JAMES ROUSE, REAL ESTATE DEVELOPER

Remembering the Facts

1. Both parents died, leaving large business debts.
2. He worked days parking cars and went to school at night.
3. A mortgage banking firm.
4. People could get inside out of the weather. They could park and walk from store to store. The malls were attractive.
5. The feeling of a village community
6. It is a lively complex of stores, restaurants, and offices.
7. It makes money by building malls and marketplaces. The money is given to the Enterprise Foundation.
8. It lends or gives money to neighborhood groups hoping to reclaim poor inner city neighborhoods.
9. The Presidential Medal of Freedom
10. Any three: housing, job training, crime reduction, school improvements, health-care improvements

Understanding the Story

Answers will vary.

11. Robin Hood took from the rich to give to the poor. The Enterprise Development Corporation gives its profits to the poor.
12. Rouse knew how to manage his business to make a good profit (the accountant and the Midas touch). He was a man on a mission to help the poor (the Sunday School teacher).

Getting the Main Idea

He saw solutions to problems in the cities which no one else had seen. He spent the last two decades of his life working to better the lives of the less fortunate.

Applying What You've Learned

Students could include snack areas, places to sit down and rest, gift wrap areas, etc.

MARY KAY ASH, COSMETICS ENTREPRENEUR

Remembering the Facts

1. Any order: a small line of products, a part-time female sales force, prizes for top sellers
2. She cared for an invalid father while her mother worked.
3. Stanley Home Products
4. While giving a Stanley "party," she met a woman who was developing creams and lotions.
5. Women received less pay than men for the same work. Also, she could not advance in the company because she was a woman.
6. "God first, family second, career third."
7. She awards them bonuses and prizes.
8. They seek to educate women on how to care for their skin, rather than selling women a product.
9. Any one: by motivating their sales force; by offering fewer products so consultants know the line well; having a good product; by keeping the price lower than the competition
10. Cancer research

Understanding the Story

Answers will vary.

11. Her mother gave her self-confidence and a competitive spirit.
12. Mary Kay Ash pays great attention to the needs of her employees. Consultants can work as little or as much as they desire. Employees are well treated. Women are given an opportunity to succeed at every level of the company.

Getting the Main Idea

Mary Kay Ash has provided an opportunity for thousands of women to better themselves and help provide for their families.

Applying What You've Learned

The script should not be a hard-sell. It should explain the benefits of the product and how to use it.

John H. Johnson, Publisher

Remembering the Facts

1. They climbed the levee, where they stayed six weeks.
2. There was no public high school for blacks in Arkansas City.
3. He was president of the senior class.
4. He was offered a part-time job by the company president, who had been the speaker at a luncheon for honor students.
5. He learned how a business works.
6. He was assigned to read magazine and newspaper articles and summarize them for his boss. He realized that blacks wanted news about community.
7. He used his mother's new furniture as collateral.
8. He was unable to obtain advertising.
9. They wanted to know the African-American point of view.
10. Economic equality

Understanding the Story

Answers will vary.

11. Gertrude insisted that he get an education. She taught him to never give up. She was willing possibly to lose her new furniture to give him a chance with his business idea.
12. Johnson never became stuck with "what worked yesterday." If an idea no longer worked, he moved on.

Getting the Main Idea

The American Dream is that anyone can succeed with hard work. Johnson came from a very disadvantaged background, but he achieved tremendous success.

Applying What You've Learned

Students should try to make their magazine appealing. Ads might be purchased by businesses that do a lot of business with teens. The cost should be low.

Fred Smith, Creator, Federal Express

Remembering the Facts

1. (a) His father died when Fred was 4.

    (b) Fred had a birth defect that made him use leg braces and crutches to walk until he was high school age.

2. Flying a plane

3. (a) It would be too expensive to get started because he would have to buy planes.
    (b) He would have to compete with the U.S. Postal Service and UPS, giant established delivery services.

4. He bought Arkansas Aviation Sales.

5. All packages are flown into a central hub. There they are sorted and flown back out on the same fleet of planes.

6. His own money, private investors, and banks to raise $90 million

7. "Absolutely, positively overnight"

8. They could buy larger planes for bigger cities and use smaller jets almost anywhere else.

9. Memphis, Tennessee

10. Electronic scanners read bar codes representing ZIP codes on the packages.

Understanding the Story

Answers will vary.

11. The ads stressed that the service provided overnight delivery and was absolutely reliable.

12. There are many occasions when people absolutely need to have something delivered on time.

Getting the Main Idea

Fred Smith saw a need for a business that no one else was able to see. He researched his idea carefully and organized his business well. He didn't give up when things were slow to work out. He has met the needs of his customers and his employees. He has created a service people can depend on.

Applying What You've Learned

Answers will vary. Following are some examples: meeting a deadline for an application; getting a present there on time; shipping medicine someone needs; shipping a part to repair a machine.

ROBERT SWANSON, BIOTECHNOLOGY SCIENTIST

Remembering the Facts

1. Biotechnology, or gene cloning
2. He and his parents decided it was the best school for him to study chemistry.
3. Bachelor's degree in chemistry and master's in business
4. He was to think of investment ideas for the firm.
5. Recombinant DNA cloning
6. Genetic engineering technology
7. From his old boss at Kleiner & Perkins, Thomas Perkins
8. Synthetic human insulin
9. It is an anti-heart attack drug. It works by dissolving clots in the arteries. It helps prevent second heart attacks.
10. They had the latest equipment and supplies. They did not have to worry about getting grants.

Understanding the Story

Answers will vary.

11. People were excited about the possibility of many more wonder drugs coming from Genentech labs. They thought they might make a big profit by buying stock.
12. Swanson was an excellent manager. Boyer was part of the team that cloned the first genes. He oversaw the labs.

Getting the Main Idea

He understood what was being done in the lab. He saw the market application of cloning before anyone else. And he had the courage to push forward with his ideas.

Applying What You've Learned

Accept any reasonable ideas. Many of the scientists would be young. They would work long hours in the lab, often at night. Dress would be casual. There would often be an air of excitement as results were near.

BEN AND JERRY, ICE-CREAM MAKERS

Remembering the Facts

1. Burlington, Vermont

2. A business which bases its decisions on its values and "gives back" to the community that supports it

3. They took a correspondence course from Penn State and then learned more by trial and error.

4. Free Cone Day

5. They weren't charging enough for their product.

6. If it isn't fun, why do it?

7. *Ben & Jerry's Double Dip*

8. Business

9. Customers and employees can become very loyal.

10. Small Business Persons of the Year

Understanding the Story

11. If values are the first priority, every decision the company makes will be based on its values. If values are an afterthought, they may be a part of what the company does if there is time or if it is convenient.

12. You influence business every time you buy a product, or refuse to buy it. You can also make your opinions known directly by calling or writing the company. You may buy stock in a company that fits with your values.

Getting the Main Idea

Ben & Jerry's puts social concerns first. Profit comes because they have earned the loyalty of their customers.

Applying What You've Learned

Students might include such things as these: writing a mission statement; basing your decisions on this mission; choosing a cause(s) you wish to support; looking out for the welfare of your employees with good pay, benefits, and working conditions; using products that are environmentally friendly.

OPRAH WINFREY, TV TALK SHOW HOST

Remembering the Facts

1. She gave her a strong religious background. She taught her to read and write.

2. She loved to memorize and recite poems quite young.

3. The home was full; she went to live with her father.

4. He gave her strict rules. He demanded she learn five new words a day and read a book each week.

5. She won a speech contest held by the Elks.

6. She could not be objective, leaving her emotions and opinions out of her reporting.

7. After she was fired as a reporter, she was given a spot cohosting a morning talk show called *People Are Talking.*

8. *The Color Purple*

9. Movies based on novels by African-American writers

10. Any two: scholarships at TSU, a tutoring program and scholarship program in a housing project, Morehouse College, Chicago Academy of the Performing Arts, battered women, AIDS

Understanding the Story

Answers will vary.

11. It was too good a chance to further her career to pass up.

12. *Pro:* At their best, talk shows give people information and help them explore issues. *Con:* Some talk shows concentrate on sensational topics. They sometimes try to make all these things "acceptable" in the name of open-mindedness.

Getting the Main Idea

Good film can make you think and expand your horizons. The movies Oprah has chosen to do all have messages to share. Her talk show seeks to do this also, and usually succeeds.

Applying What You've Learned

Examples: More college prep courses should be offered at our school. Drugs are a problem at our school.

BILL GATES, FOUNDER OF MICROSOFT

Remembering the Facts

1. A teletype machine (an ASR-33) that was linked to a computer in a business in downtown Seattle

2. It was a company set up by Gates and Paul Allen to interpret data about traffic patterns.

3. A version of the computer language BASIC that allowed a person to communicate with the machine

4. He knew the time was right to go into the computer software business.

5. A combination of the words *microcomputer* and *software*.

6. An operating system (MS-DOS) and BASIC software for the IBM PC

7. Gates insisted on retaining ownership of MS-DOS and the software. IBM had to pay him royalties on each PC sold with the operating system and software.

8. The company went public; large amounts of stock were sold.

9. The value of the stock went sky high.

10. Any three: MS-DOS, Windows, Word for Windows, EXCEL, Internet Explorer, Microsoft Mouse, etc.

Understanding the Story

Answers will vary.

11. His wealth keeps growing mostly because of the skyrocketing price of Microsoft stock. Royalties from Microsoft products, sales of software, new businesses bought, and royalties from IBM-PC's sold with the Microsoft operating system all push up the price of stock.

12. He is quick to see and take advantage of an opportunity. He thinks things through quickly and fully. He works hard for very long hours. He loves what he does.

Getting the Main Idea

Thomas Edison was the inventor of the light bulb and about 1,000 other electrical products. Gates has made computers an everyday part of the lives of millions of Americans. Both have made inventions that have changed how many people live.

Applying What You've Learned

Accept any reasonable idea. Students should have specific tasks for their computer program to do.

JERRY YANG, DEVELOPER, YAHOO!

Remembering the Facts

1. Taiwan

2. He spoke no English other than the word *shoe*.

3. They were Ph.D. students in electrical engineering at Stanford.

4. Their faculty advisor was in Europe on sabbatical.

5. It is arranged in a hierarchy of categories. At the top are 14 broad categories. These become more specific as one browses down through the levels.

6. It was a free service to its users.

7. Koogle was to manage the business end of Yahoo!

8. Any two: ads, news service, weather service, stock quotes

9. The company went public.

10. It is a personalized web page with easy access to all the sites the person likes to use.

Understanding the Story

Answers will vary.

11. Yahoo! is a "cool" search engine. Its founders are young. They do not charge for their service. Yahoo! is easy to use.

12. They did not want to be told what to do. They had created Yahoo! and wanted to be in charge of how it developed.

Getting the Main Idea

Yang and Filo started Yahoo! as a hobby. It developed into an obsession the two worked on day and night. Yang enjoys Yahoo! so much that he thinks working on it is fun.

Applying What You've Learned

Answers will vary.

Additional Activities

Frederic Tudor: the Ice King
1. Read more information on methods of ice harvesting.
2. Read about the history of ice cream.
3. Find out about the development of modern refrigeration.

Biddy Mason: Philanthropist
1. Read William Katz' book *Black Women of the Old West* to learn about other African-American women in the old West.
2. Write to the Chamber of Commerce of Los Angeles for more information about Biddy Mason Park or the Broadway Spring Center.

Andrew Carnegie: Steel Industrialist
1. Find out about the Bessemer process for producing steel.
2. Read about the development of the telegraph system by Samuel B. Morse.
3. Read about the story of the transcontinental railroad, ending at Promontory Point, Utah, in 1869.
4. Find out about the life of J.P. Morgan, financier.
5. Find out about the work of the Carnegie Foundation today.
6. Find out more about Carnegie-Mellon University in Pittsburgh.
7. Read about one of the major steel companies in the United States today: Bethlehem Steel, U.S. Steel, for example.

Montgomery Ward: Catalog Sales Wizard
1. Find out more about the history of other giant retailers offering catalog sales, such as Sears or J. C. Penney.

2. Obtain a mail-order catalog. Write a paragraph describing its contents, shipping policies, return policies, etc.
3. Find out more about Montgomery Ward Company today.

King Gillette: Inventor of the Safety Razor

1. Gillette's mother was the author of *The White House Cook Book,* published in 1887. A bestseller, it was revised and updated many times, most recently in 1976. Find a copy of the cookbook and share it with the class.
2. Read and report on one of King Gillette's books, *The World Corporation* or *The Human Drift.*
3. Find out more about the 1871 Chicago fire.
4. Find out about the Gillette Company, its products, and financial health.
5. Report on another socialist writer, such as Edward Bellamy, Jack London, or Ignatius Donnelly.
6. Take a trip to the grocery store or drug store. List the shaving products made by the Gillette Company. Compare your lists as a class.

Henry Ford: Automotive Pioneer

1. Read about Edsel Ford, Henry Ford's son.
2. Find out about Henry Ford II, grandson of Henry Ford.
3. Read about the development of other car companies, such as Dodge, Chevrolet, or Jeep.
4. Find out what work the Ford Foundation does.
5. Read about the Ford Motor Company today. What cars does it make? What is the financial strength of the company?
6. Compare America's love affair with the Model T to its much later love for the VW Beetle.

Madam C.J. Walker: Hair-Care Innovator

1. Read more about Madam C.J. Walker's life.
2. One of Madam Walker's favorite charities was Bethune-Cookman College. Find out more about the life of Mary McLeod Bethune. (Read Bethune's story in *16 Extraordinary African Americans* by J. Weston Walch, Publisher.)
3. Read more about the glory days of Harlem in the early 1900's.
4. Read about the life of Booker T. Washington, founder of Tuskegee Institute. (Read Washington's story in *16 Extraordinary African Americans* by J. Weston Walch, Publisher.)
5. Walker worked to make lynching and mob violence a federal crime. Find out more about the race riots against black people from 1917 to 1919.

6. Madam Walker's mansion, Villa Lewaro, is being made into a museum. Write for information to the Villa at North Broadway Avenue, Irvington-on-Hudson, New York 10533.

7. The Walker Building in Indianapolis housed her factory, offices, and the biggest movie house in Indianapolis. Today it is the Madame C.J. Walker Urban Life Center. Write for more information to the Center, at 617 Indiana Avenue, Indianapolis, Indiana 46202 (telephone: 317-236-2099).

James Rouse: Real Estate Developer

1. Find out more about Rouse's planned city: Columbia, Maryland. Write a brief description of the city. Explain whether you would like to live there.

2. If you have visited a festival marketplace, report on it to the class. Did you enjoy it? Why or why not?

Mary Kay Ash: Cosmetics Entrepreneur

1. Read one of Mary Kay Ash's books. (See "References" for a list.)

2. Locate a Mary Kay consultant. Have her give a brief presentation to the class about the work she does.

3. Read about what Mary Kay Cosmetics, Inc., is doing today.

John H. Johnson: Publisher

1. Find out more about the flood of 1927.

2. Obtain a copy of *Ebony* or *Jet* at a newsstand or library. Read it to see what types of articles and advertisements it contains.

3. Read Johnson's autobiography, *Succeeding Against the Odds*.

4. Find out the current status of Johnson's various companies.

5. Find out what Johnson Publishing Company is doing today.

6. Go to a department store and look to see if they carry the Fashion Fair cosmetics line. If so, find out what types of products are included in the line.

Fred Smith: Creator, Federal Express

1. Federal Express has a student packet with information about its history and services. Contact them at www.fedex.com.

2. Find out what Fred Smith is doing today.

3. Read the stories of other delivery services: Emory Air Freight, United Parcel Service or the U.S. Postal Service.

4. Read about Juan Trippe, founder of Pan American Airways.

Robert Swanson: Biotechnology Scientist

1. Find out what Genentech is doing today. What new medicines have been released?
2. Read about what Robert Swanson is doing today.
3. Read the stories of other giant drug companies: Eli Lilly, Merck, Hoffman-La Roche, Bristol Myers Squibb, etc.
4. Read more about Watson and Crick's discoveries in the book *The Double Helix.*
5. Find out more about genetic engineering techniques.

Ben and Jerry: Ice-Cream Makers

1. Read the book *Ben & Jerry's Double Dip.*
2. Read *Value Line* for an analytical look at Ben & Jerry's.
3. Buy some Ben & Jerry's Ice Cream and try it for yourself!

Oprah Winfrey: TV Talk Show Host

1. Read Oprah's book: *The Uncommon Wisdom of Oprah.*
2. Tune in to Oprah's show one day. Write a brief report telling whether you think the show made a positive contribution that day. Give reasons for your opinion.
3. Watch *The Oprah Winfrey Show* and another TV talk show. Compare and contrast the two shows in content and tone.
4. Watch a movie produced by HARPO Productions, Inc. Some are *The Women of Brewster Place, Beloved, Kaffir Boy, There Are No Children Here,* and *Their Eyes Were Watching God.*

Bill Gates: Founder of Microsoft

1. Read a copy of Gates' book *The Road Ahead.*
2. Find Microsoft on the Internet (www.microsoft.com).
3. Find out what Bill Gates is doing today.
4. Get a copy of this year's *Forbes* list of the 400 richest people in America. Find out where Gates is on the list.
5. Visit a computer store. Make a list of some of the software programs that are made by Microsoft.

Jerry Yang: Developer, Yahoo!

1. Read about other net services such as Excite and Lycos.
2. Find out how Yahoo! is doing today.
3. Read about what Jerry Yang and David Filo are doing today.
4. Access Yahoo! and see how it is constructed.

References

Frederic Tudor: the Ice King

Rembert, S.S. "Artificial Ice, the South." *Scientific American,* July 22, 1854, page 80.

Cummings, Richard O. *The American Ice Harvests: A Historical Study in Technology, 1800–1918.* Berkeley, CA: 1949.

"Frederic Tudor—Ice King." *Bulletin of the Business Historical Society,* 6 (4), September 1932, pp. 1–8.

"Ice Cultivation." *Scientific American,* November 29, 1851.

Sobel, Robert, and David B. Sicilia. *The Entrepreneurs: An American Adventure.* Boston: Houghton Mifflin Company, 1986, pp. 65–71.

Biddy Mason: Philanthropist

Hine, Diane Clark, ed. *Black Women in America. Vol. II.* New York: Carlson Publishers, Inc., 1993, pp. 753-754.

Igus, Toyomi, ed. *Great Women in the Struggle.* New Jersey: Just Us Books, 1991, page 69.

Hayden, Dolores. "Biddy Mason's Los Angeles, 1856-1891." *California History* 68 (Fall l989), pp. 86–99.

Smith, Jessie Carney, ed. *Notable Black American Women.* Detroit: Gale Research, 1992.

Andrew Carnegie: Steel Industrialist

Bowman, John. *Andrew Carnegie: Steel Tycoon.* Englewood Cliffs, NJ: Silver Burdett Press, 1989.

Judson, Clara Ingram. *Andrew Carnegie.* Chicago: Follett Publishing Co., 1964.

Shippen, Katherine. *Andrew Carnegie and the Age of Steel.* New York: Random House, 1958.

Montgomery Ward: Catalog Sales Wizard

Herndon, Booton. *Satisfaction Guaranteed: An Unconventional Report to Today's Consumers.* New York: McGraw-Hill Co., 1972.

Latham, Frank Brown. *1872–1972: A Century of Serving Consumers. The Story of Montgomery Ward.* Chicago: Montgomery Ward, 1972.

Sobel, Robert, and David B. Sicilia. *The Entrepreneurs: An American Adventure.* Boston: Houghton Mifflin Company, 1986, pp. 209-211.

"The History of Montgomery Ward." On the Internet at www.mward.com 1998.

Weil, Gordon L. *Sears, Roebuck, U.S.A.* New York: Stein & Day Publishers, 1977.

King Gillette: Inventor of the Safety Razor

Adams, Russell B. *King C. Gillette, The Man and His Wonderful Shaving Device.* Boston: Little, Brown and Company, 1978.

Sobel, Robert, and David B. Sicilia. *The Entrepreneurs: An American Adventure.* Boston: Houghton Mifflin Co., 1986, pp 16–20.

Henry Ford: Automotive Pioneer

Collier, Peter, and David Horowitz. *The Fords.* New York: Summit Books, 1987.

Kelly, Regina Z. *Henry Ford.* Chicago: Follett Publishing Co., 1970.

Quackenbush, Robert. *Along Came the Model T.* New York: Parents' Magazine Press, 1978.

Sobel, Robert, and David B. Sicila. *The Entrepreneurs: An American Adventure.* Boston: Houghton Mifflin Co., 1986, pp. 170–8.

Wik, Reynold M. *Henry Ford and Grass-Roots America.* Ann Arbor, MI: The University of Michigan Press, 1972.

Madam C.J. Walker: Hair-Care Innovator

Bundles, A'Lelia Perry. *Madam C.J. Walker.* New York: Chelsea House Publishers, 1991.

Colman, Penny. *Madam C.J. Walker.* Brookfield, CT: The Millbrook Press, 1994.

Forbes, Malcolm. *Women Who Made a Difference.* New York: Simon & Schuster, 1990, pp. 299-301.

Taylor, Marian W. *Madam C.J. Walker, Pioneer Businesswoman.* New York: Chelsea House Publishers, 1994.

James Rouse: Real Estate Developer

Goldberger, Paul. "James W. Rouse, 81, Dies; Socially Conscious Developer Built Towns and Malls." *New York Times,* April 16, 1996.

Griffith-Roberts, Carolanne. "Building with a Vision," *Southern Living,* June 1990, pp. 46–54.

"James W(ilson) Rouse." *Current Biography.* New York: The H.T. Wilson Company, 1982, pp. 374-8.

Jones, Malcolm Jr. "James Rouse Sparked New Life in Old Cities." *Newsweek,* April 22, 1996, page 78.

Meyer, Michael. *The Alexander Complex: The Dreams That Drive the Great Businessmen.* New York: Times Books, 1989.

Zoglin, Richard. "The Urban Renewer: James W. Rouse: 1914–1996." *Time,* April 22, 1996.

Mary Kay Ash: Cosmetics Entrepreneur

Ash, Mary Kay. *Mary Kay on People Management.* New York: Warner Books, Inc., 1984.

Ash, Mary Kay. *Mary Kay: The Story of America's Most Dynamic Businesswoman.* New York: Harper & Row Publishers, 1981.

Ash, Mary Kay. *You Can Have It All.* Rocklin, CA: Prima Pub., 1995.

John H. Johnson: Publisher

Falkof, Lucille. *John H. Johnson: The Man from Ebony.* Ada, OK: Garrett Educational Corporation, 1992.

John H. Johnson. *Succeeding against the Odds.* New York: Warner Books, 1989.

Fred Smith: Creator, Federal Express

Ingram, John N., and Lynne B. Feldman. "Frederick Wallace Smith." In *Contemporary American Business Leaders.* New York: Greenwood Press, 1990.

Sobel, Robert, and David B. Sicila. *The Entrepreneurs: An American Adventure.* Boston: Houghton Mifflin Co., 1986, pp. 42–48.

Robert Swanson: Bioengineering Scientist

Hamilton, Joan O'C. "Biotech's First Superstar." *Business Week,* April 14, 1986, pp. 68–72.

Hamilton, Joan O'C. "Why Genentech Ditched the Dream of Independence." *Business Week,* February 19, 1990, pp. 36–37.

Meyer, Michael. *The Alexander Complex: The Dreams that Drive Great Businessmen.* New York: Times Books, 1989.

Ben and Jerry: Ice–Cream Makers

Cohen, Ben, and Jerry Greenfield. *Ben & Jerry's Double Dip.* New York: Simon & Schuster, 1997.

Greenberg, Keith. *Ben and Jerry: Ice Cream for Everyone.* Woodbridge, CT: Blackbirch Press, 1994.

Lager, Fred "Chico." *Ben and Jerry's: The Inside Scoop.* New York: Crown Publishers, 1994.

Oprah Winfrey: TV Talk Show Host

Beaton, Margaret. *Oprah Winfrey: TV Talk Show Host.* Chicago: Children's Press, 1990.

Bly, Nellie. *Oprah: Up Close and Down Home.* New York: Zebra Books, 1993.

Mair, George. *Oprah Winfrey: The Real Story.* New York: Carol Publishing Group, 1994.

Pope, Kyle. "The Talk of TV: Oprah Stays, King World Pays." *The Wall Street Journal,* September 16, 1997, page B1.

Saidman, Anne. *Oprah Winfrey: Media Success Story.* Minneapolis: Lerner Publications, 1990.

Woods, Geraldine. *The Oprah Winfrey Story: Speaking Her Mind.* Minneapolis, MN: 1991.

Bill Gates: Founder of Microsoft

Dickinson, Joan D. *Bill Gates: Billionaire Computer Genius.* Springfield, NJ: Enslow Publishers, Inc., 1997.

Conlin, Michelle. "The Forbes Four Hundred." *Forbes,* October 13, 1997, page 152.

Gates, William. *The Road Ahead.* New York: Viking Penguin, 1995.

Ingram, John N., and Lynne B. Feldman. *Contemporary American Business Leaders.* New York: Greenwood Press, 1990, pp. 162–6.

Walters, Barbara. "An Interview with Bill Gates." On television's "20/20", January 30, 1998.

Jerry Yang: Developer, Yahoo!

"Jerry Yang," *Current Biography.* New York: The H.W. Wilson Co., October 1997, pp. 54–7.

"Jerry Yang, Chief Yahoo." *Forbes ASAP,* December 1, 1997.

Reid, Robert H. *Architects of the Web.* New York: John Wiley & Sons, Inc., 1997.